THINK WELL ON IT

"The kingdom of heaven suffereth violence, and the violent bear it away."
—Matthew 11:12

THINK WELL ON IT

REFLECTIONS ON THE GREAT TRUTHS
OF THE CATHOLIC RELIGION

By

Bishop Richard Challoner
(1691-1781)

*"With desolation is all the land made
desolate, because there is none that considereth in the heart."*
—Jeremias 12:11

TAN BOOKS AND PUBLISHERS, INC.
Rockford, Illinois 61105

This 2006 complete edition from TAN Books and Publishers, Inc. of *Think Well On It* has been taken from the unabridged edition of 1842 printed by Richardson and Son, Derby, England, that was published by the Catholic Book Society, under the title *Think Well On't: Or Reflections on the Great Truths of the Christian Religion for Every Day in the Year* with a then new Preface and some additional concluding prayers added. This entire edition has been retypeset and re-published using Bishop Challoner's complete text, but adding very minor editing and a fairly major updating of language, plus some additional Scripture passages which were alluded to by the author but not quoted, or not quoted completely, in Bishop Challoner's original work.

ISBN 0-89555-763-0

Printed and bound in the United States of America.

TAN Books and Publishers, Inc.
P.O. Box 424
Rockford, Illinois 61105
2006

Dedicated
To The Blessed Virgin Mary

"Consider . . . that part that the Blessed Virgin Mother bore in the sufferings of her Son and how truly was here verified that prophecy of the aged Simeon: *"And thy own soul a sword shall pierce."* (*Luke* 2:35). Oh, how killing a grief must have oppressed this most tender and most loving of all mothers when—during the whole course of the Passion of her dearest Son, whom she loved with an incomparable love—she was an eyewitness to all the injuries, outrages and torments that He endured. Ah, Blessed Lady, may we not truly say that the whips, thorns and nails that pierced thy Son's flesh made so deep a wound in thy virginal heart that nothing but a miracle could have supported thy life under such excess of pain? But oh, what a deep wound didst thou feel in thy soul when thy dying Son recommended thee to His Beloved Disciple St. John, giving to thee the son of Zebedee in exchange for the Son of God! Blessed Virgin, we gladly acknowledge thee for our Mother, bequeathed to us all in the person of St. John. Oh, by all thy sufferings, remember us poor banished children of Eve before the Throne of Grace! Christians, learn the admirable lessons which Our Lady teaches you at the foot of the Cross. Learn her unshaken faith and undoubted hope. Learn her perfect resignation, patience and fortitude! Oh, learn from her to love Jesus and detest sin, the true cause of all His sufferings!" —Page 108.

Publisher's Preface

THINK Well On It—small book that it is—nonetheless is probably the most powerful admonition that exists in the English language for us to heed the words of the Gospel, rectify our lives, and begin in earnest the serious job of working out our salvation. It makes an ideal spiritual exercise, and should be reread every year for several years running, and thereafter at least every three years or so for the rest of one's life, in order to keep before one's mind the principles, truths and urgings that are so cogently and succinctly marshalled up in these relatively few pages.

Except for the Blessed Virgin Mary, who never committed even the smallest sin, the rest of mankind are sinners. And even the St. Joseph edition of *Baltimore Catechism Number 2* (for sixth through eighth graders) says very forthrightly that most adults commit mortal sin. Those who would deny this fact need only reflect for a moment that most Catholics today are regularly missing Mass on Sunday. As of this writing, the current statistic is that only 25 percent of Catholics in the U.S. attend Sunday Mass. In some Western countries the percentage is far worse. It is a mortal sin for Catholics willfully to miss Mass on Sunday. Critics of this view about the percentage of adults who commit mortal sin should also reflect on the shameless discussion of sexuality in our society, plus the rampant immodesty in dress and the open portrayal in films and T.V. productions of people committing illicit sexual acts. Combined with godless sex education in our schools, these factors have largely contributed to the openly acknowledged "sexual revolution" that blossomed in the 1960's and has continued apace since then. The Catholic Church teaches that all sexual activity—other than that allowed between husband and wife that is left open to procreation—is a mortal sin, which also includes even thoughts about such illicit actions that are entertained willfully and taken pleasure in. Our Lady of Fatima said that more souls go to Hell for sins of the flesh than for any other reason, and St. Alphonsus Liguori (1696-1787), a Doctor of the Church, said that the Fathers and Doctors of the Church and holy writers are unanimous in the opinion that of those who go to Hell, 90 percent go there because of sins of impurity (sexual sins). Then too, we should consider the powerful statement of St. Peter, Prince of the Apostles, when he said, *"If the just shall scarcely be saved, where shall the ungodly and the sinner appear?"* (*1 Peter* 4:18). (Here the "just" refers to those who are in the state of grace and who are presumably striving diligently to save their souls.) Therefore, it can easily be concluded that the great majority of people—Catholic and non-Catholic alike—are not in the state of grace and therefore are on the path to Hell, and therefore truly need the assistance of this book, or something comparable, to help motivate them to rectify their lives.

As the author points out here in several places, *now*, while we are living, is the time for God's mercy; after we die, we shall have to face His justice and accept what we have deserved by our lives. Many who read this book will probably become nay-sayers and deny that God would hold human beings to such strict standards as indicated here. But the fact is that all of what the author presents to us is taken from Scripture, and most of it from the Gospels and out of the very mouth of Our Divine Saviour Himself. Even He has admonished us: *"Be you therefore perfect, as also your heavenly Father is perfect."* (*Matthew* 5:48). We all know that no one who is imperfect will enter Heaven. The inescapable conclusion, therefore, is that we are all going to have to work diligently to become perfect, if we plan to save our souls and hopefully avoid Purgatory.

Those who would say that the Catholic Church no

longer teaches such a strict doctrine as presented in this book are really forced into rejecting Jesus Christ and the Gospel itself, for as the author demonstrates, Our Lord will hold us to a strict account for all of our actions. *"But I say unto you, that every idle word that men shall speak, they shall render an account for it in the day of judgment."* (*Matthew* 12:36). Those who would deny this teaching would have to reject the Bible, plus nearly 2000 years of Catholic Tradition. In effect, they would have to deny Christ. Many in the Church today have fallen victim to the heresy of Modernism, which in essence is *relativism,* the belief that truth changes with man's perception of the truth. In his famous 1907 encyclical *Pascendi Dominici Gregis (Against Modernism)*, Pope St. Pius X (1903-1914) condemned Modernism formally as a heresy, calling it the "summation of all errors."

People who have been virtuous all their lives and have avoided mortal sin from their youth, while they undoubtedly do not deny the strictness of the Faith, may nonetheless say that this book is too strong for them. Such good people need to realize several important truths: 1) *Anyone* can fall into mortal sin, which usually happens when one becomes lax about practicing the Faith and about committing venial sin, which often leads one gradually to commit mortal sin. 2) Even those who are making definite progress toward perfection should realize that the spirit of sin remains in all of us and at all times, and that we must all constantly war against it and will have to do so our entire lives—right up to and including the time of our death. 3) The majority of adults are living in mortal sin—or at least are committing them regularly, even though they may be repenting. For all these reasons, therefore, everyone needs to read this book—for the truly good, to remind them of the strict accounting we are all going to have to make of our lives; and for the lax, to alert them to the great danger they are in of losing their souls.

The author calls this a book of *considerations*, and says

that "the lack of consideration of the great truths of Christianity is the chief source of all our evils." Therefore, this is a book to be read carefully and reflected upon, one to be read over and over again, to be prayed over and thought about deeply. It is not a book solely of information, but rather, and more particularly, of *formation;* it is not a book just to be read and then for the reader to pass on to the next book and the next and the next. Some books deserve to be read only once, but not this one. (It would be an excellent practice to make this book one's *vade mecum*, or "travelling companion," and to read from it daily, either as part of one's morning meditations or before retiring in the evening.)

St. Paul tells us, *"It is appointed unto men once to die, and after this the judgment."* (*Hebrews* 9:27). Once we die, it is too late to do anything further toward our salvation. If we miss saving our souls, it will then be too late for us. As the author states here, we have no chance to rehearse for this singular and all-important event. But *now,* while we are living, is the time of God's mercy; *now* is the time for conversion; *now* is the time to work out our salvation. Again, to quote St. Paul, *"Behold,* now *is the acceptable time; behold,* now *is the day of salvation."* (*2 Corinthians* 6:2, emphasis added). Yes, Dear Reader, *now* is the time to work out your salvation; *now* is the time to get serious about saving your soul; *now* is the time of God's mercy; *now* He has allotted you a certain segment of time in which to rectify your life and show Him that you love Him. When you die, it will be too late for action on your part; then you will have to accept what you have merited. But the mercy of God taken advantage of *now* enables everyone of us to erase the sins of our past and to pay, at a very small price indeed, for the temporal punishment that is due to them. But we need to begin the job *now* of rectifying our lives and paying back in prayer, penance, good works and almsgiving for the spiritual damage that our sins have done. You break someone's window, and it is usually easy to obtain his forgiveness, but you still have to pay for the window. Spiritually speaking, most of us have broken a good many windows, and we need to start *now* to pay for them, yes, *now,* when we shall pay with a nickel what in Purgatory will cost us 10 thousand dollars—according to a revelation of St. Marianne of Quito (1618-1645).

This book may cause a person feelings of despair over his salvation, especially if he has heretofore not led a good life. We must all adopt a middle course in the evaluation of our spiritual lives—between, on the one hand, *presumption* of our salvation and, on the other, *despair* at the danger of losing it. Each of these extremes is a sin and is to be avoided. Considering the generality of mankind today, one would have to judge that most people sin by *presumption* that they will be saved—for without ever really investigating what are the *terms* for salvation, they proceed to lead spiritually lax, sloppy lives. It is a doctrine of the Catholic Church that no one is *certain* whether or not he be in the state of grace and therefore worthy of salvation. (Council of Trent: Session 6, Chapter 9). Scripture puts the teaching this way: *"Man knoweth not whether he be worthy of love or hatred."* (*Ecclesiastes* 9:1). Though we all definitely need to be seriously concerned over our spiritual condition, there is no purpose to be served in simply becoming *anxious* about it, or *scrupulous* (where one sees everything as a sin, which tends to neutralize a person from making sound moral judgments). Rather than develop a useless anxiety or lapse into confusing scruples, a person should be humble (that is to say, *realistic*) about truly rectifying his life, become thoroughly instructed in the Faith, pray regularly and with devotion, seek the advice of a good confessor or spiritual director, examine his conscience daily, go to Confession often, "at least once a week" (in the words of St. Alphonsus Liguori), attend Mass and receive Holy Communion often and devoutly, say his morning and evening prayers faithfully, recite at least five decades of the Rosary each day (Our Lady's Fatima request) and consecrate himself to the Sacred Heart of Jesus and the Blessed Virgin Mary. Earning our eternal salvation (with the help of God's grace) is the biggest job we shall ever undertake. Therefore, we need to shoulder the task intelligently, earnestly and with determination. If a Catholic informs himself about his religious duties and uses the spiritual assistance Our Lord has provided through the Catholic Church—the Mass, Sacraments, sacramentals, priestly counsel, prayer, etc.—the job becomes much lighter and is an actual joy, because he has a clear conscience and *realizes* he is on the path to salvation. *"Take up my yoke upon you and learn of me, because I am meek and humble of heart, and you shall find rest to your souls. For my yoke is sweet and my burden light."* (*Matthew* 11:29-30).

This book calls for us to get serious about our salvation, but most people, from what has been said above, are not. Most people are casual about saving their souls, lukewarm, but lukewarmness will not get the job done. Witness what Our Lord says in the *Apocalypse*: *"Because thou art lukewarm, and neither cold nor hot, I will begin to vomit thee out of my mouth."* (*Apocalypse* 3:16). Notice that He says *"begin* to vomit," and not categorically that He will do so. So there is still hope for the lukewarm. Lukewarmness obviously disgusts and nauseates Him, comparable to a meal that has soured in one's stomach, with which there is nothing to do but vomit it out. Imagine the infinite intelligence of our Divine Lord, who nonetheless chose this most disgusting human experience to describe how He considers those who are lukewarm. But again, the lukewarm *still* have a chance—"I will *begin* to vomit thee out of my mouth." He has not done so yet; while we live, there is still time to reform, but the rejection is eventually coming, unless we change, for we shall otherwise die in our lukewarmness! And why shall we fail to save our souls if we are lukewarm? *Because we are not really trying!* And this tepidity on our part must totally disgust Our Lord after His undergoing

His incredible and to us unimaginable Passion and Death. He has shown so much love for us and so much concern for us as to undergo what can only be described as a superhuman effort in his Agony and Death. Presumably, most people have seen Mel Gibson's film *The Passion of the Christ,* and most were so moved by it they do not want to witness it again. Yet by his own admission, Mel Gibson says this film is not anywhere near so harsh and brutal as the actual Passion and Death undergone by Our Lord and described by the Catholic visionaries Bl. Anne Catherine Emmerich, Ven. Mary of Agreda, St. Bridget of Sweden, Therese Neumann, St. Claire of Montefalco, and others.

Why would Our Lord have put Himself through such an agony when He could have done something far, far less traumatic, e.g., pricked His little finger with a pin, shed a drop of blood and said, "There, that redeems you. My Father is satisfied." But no, He chose instead to undergo probably the greatest suffering any human being has ever experienced and to die in the most ignominious manner possible. For what reason? For several reasons: 1) To show us forcefully and demonstratively the seriousness of sin, that it can and will send us to Hell for all eternity if we die unrepentant; 2) to show us that salvation is a *big* job; 3) to demonstrate just how much He loves us, is willing to do for us, and has *already* done for us. Hell is a stark reality according to Our Lord's teaching. He has told us it is better to pluck out an eye or cut off one of our hands, if these are an occasion of sin for us, rather than to go into Hell and be lost forever. Moreover, Our Lord has revealed to a number of Saints and holy people that He would be willing to undergo His entire Passion and Death all over again—*for each one of us*—if that is what it would take to effect each person's salvation! In the face of such sacrificial love, a love that is incomprehensible to us, our lukewarmness would indeed be disgusting to Him.

Think Well On It was published in 1728 when Bishop Challoner was about 37 years old. It was his first book after his doctoral dissertation had been written. The edition that this book was adapted from was published in 1842 and claims to be complete and unabridged. Therefore, 278 years have elapsed between the first appearance of this book and this present edition in 2006. Much change occurs in a language during that length of time, and consequently a fairly good deal of updating to the words had to be done to make the book perfectly clear and easy to read in our time. Also, the method of punctuating is markedly different today from what it was then. The original book was simply filled with unnecessary commas; plus, colons were used extensively, the exact purpose of which is difficult to determine. Bishop Challoner, as with so many people with a classical education, frequently employed long sentences. These often had to be read and reread many times in order to punctuate them correctly, so that the meaning would be made completely clear.

Because this book was written *before* Bishop Challoner updated the Douay-Rheims Bible (in 1749, 1750 and 1752), his Bible quotes in the original edition of *Think Well On It* did not correspond exactly to the Douay-Rheims. Care has been taken to convert all the Bible quotes in this edition to the familiar Douay-Rheims version. Oftentimes too, he would not quote quite the entire applicable passage; for this edition we have supplied these sayings in their entirety as they are typically quoted. Also at times, the author would allude to certain Scriptural passages, or he would use phrases therefrom, but without citing chapter, verse or source. For this edition, the complete Bible quotes have often simply been added to the text without using brackets to show that they have been added. In some cases, very light editing of the text itself was done to make the flow better and easier to understand. Bishop Challoner used both the "thee-thou-thine" personal pronoun and adjective form and the "you-your." Both uses have been retained here in an effort to maintain the tenor and tone of the original book, as well as to leave the book with its original flavor of holiness, spiritual unction and time-lessness.

The title of the book originally was *Think Well On't.* Because we do not use *on't* as a contraction anymore, the title was changed to what it is here. Oftentimes the author would simply use the word "grace" when he was referring to Sanctifying Grace; we chose to use the latter for perfect clarity. Bishop Challoner published this book when the Penal Laws of Great Britain against Catholics were still in effect and being enforced in some places and by some officers of the law. (For many years as Coadjutor Bishop of London, he had to change his residence every year and could not wear his clerical garb.) This book appeared in 1728, before he returned to England in 1730. Whether he had the book typeset and published on the Continent or in England, one still has to wonder if, under such circumstances, he had a competent Catholic editor to go over this book before publication. Few authors indeed are able to produce a manuscript that is perfect and ready for printing without the help of an editor to clean up small details of rhetoric and punctuation. These matters have all been taken care of in this present edition.

Had *Think Well On It* been reprinted exactly as the 1842 edition of the complete and unabridged work and without the changes made here, it would probably have had a far lower readership and have much less impact, due to the difficulty of the older language and the cumbersomeness of the overpunctuation. From the inception of our work on this book to its final layout, I have personally taken charge of modernizing *Think Well On It,* and have either made or approved all of the changes myself. Mary Frances Lester, a very experienced and highly talented editor at TAN, assisted by making numerous helpful suggestions that have greatly improved readibility.

This book is not being republished for antiquarian or historic purposes, but rather to inspire the reader with the spirit of our Faith that is breathed into every line of this incomparable work by its learned and pious author. Despite the extensive updating of words, the elimination of gross overpunctuation and some light editing, *Think Well On It* nonetheless *remains* completely Bishop Richard Challoner's book, and I believe it is now in as good an updated and yet complete version as can possibly be given to the modern reader. Personally, I think it simply sparkles with the truth of our Catholic Faith. It is our fond hope that the reader will agree.

—Thomas A. Nelson
Publisher
March 9, 2006
St. Frances of Rome
St. Dominic Savio

Preface to the 1842 Edition

ALTHOUGH the following little work may be perused by all with profit, even by those long accustomed to set apart a certain portion of their time daily to pious reading and who have made no small progress in the ways of an interior life, yet by none have its exceeding merits been more clearly recognized than by such as have been awakened, whether on a sickbed or in health, to a sense of sinful habits, and who have sought for some simple book to feed and strengthen those first desires to amend their lives, inspired by the grace of God. How many in humble life may date their conversion from the hour in which this book was first put into their hands! And how many, required when children by their pastors and parents to read it, and who may have been unhappily afterwards led astray for years by their passions and the corruption of general bad example, have recollected with emotion the pious sentiments with which this book once inspired them, and have sought it again as containing the best motives and encouragements to return and ask forgiveness of their heavenly Father!

In this edition there have been added the *Penitent's Litany*, and the *Instruction and Prayers in Time of Sickness*, extracted from the ninth volume of Gother. Might not this book be used occasionally as a reading book in our schools for the poor? The child possessed of a Catechism, Prayer Book and *Think Well On It* has a good library, and if instructed and guided by the spirit of these books, is far wiser than very many having thousands of volumes.

Directions for the Use of
The Following Considerations

1. Make choice of a proper time and place for recollection, and shut the door of your heart as much as possible against the world and its distracting cares and affections.

2. Place yourself in the presence of your God, representing Him to yourself by a lively faith as filling Heaven and earth with His incomprehensible Majesty, or as residing with all His attributes in the very center of your own soul. Prostrate yourself in spirit before Him to adore this sovereign LORD; make an offering of your whole self unto Him and humbly beg pardon for all your past treasons against Him.

3. Implore with fervor and humility His light and grace, that the great truths of the Gospel may make a due impression on your soul, in order that you may effectually learn to fear Him and to love Him.

4. Read leisurely and with serious attention the chapter for the day; give your soul time to digest what you are reading, and pause more particularly on those points which affect you most.

5. That your reading may partake more of the nature of mental prayer, strive to draw from your considerations such affections as are suitable to the subject by stirring up, for example, in your soul the fear and love of God,

a confidence in His goodness, a sense of gratitude for His benefits, the horror of sin, a sincere repentance for your own past sins, and similar affections; open your heart as much as you can to these affections, that thus these great and necessary virtues may take deeper root there.

6. Conclude your considerations with holy resolutions of amendment of life, insisting in particular on the failings to which you are most subject; and firmly determine within yourself to begin to put these resolutions into execution upon such occasions as may occur that very day.

7. Reflect often during the day on the chief points of your consideration, lest the enemy rob your soul of this divine seed by making you quickly forget what you have been reading and considering.

Contents

THINK WELL ON IT

"In all thy works remember thy last end, and thou shalt never sin."
—Ecclesiasticus 7:40

Chapter 1

On the Necessity of Consideration

The First Day

CONSIDER FIRST those words of the Prophet Jeremias, *"With desolation is all the land made desolate, because there is none that considereth in the heart."* (*Jeremias* 12:11). And reflect how true it is that the lack of consideration of the great truths of Christianity is the chief source of all our evils! Alas, the greatest part of mankind seldom, or never, think of either their first beginning or of their last end! Neither do they consider who brought them into the world, or for what; nor do they reflect on that eternity into which they are just about to step. Hence, all their pursuits are earthly and temporal, as if they were made only for this life, or were always to be here. Death, Judgment, Heaven and Hell make but little impression upon them because they do not give themselves the leisure to delve deeply into their souls by means of serious consideration. They run on, with their eyes shut, to the precipice of a miserable eternity; and only then do they begin to think, when they find themselves lodged in that place of woe, *"Where their worm dieth not and the fire is not extinguished."* (*Mark* 9:43). Ah, my Poor Soul, take care that this be not thy case!

Consider secondly that we cannot be saved without knowing God and loving Him above all things. Now we can neither know Him nor love Him as we ought without

1

the help of consideration. It is this which reveals to us
the infinite perfections of this Sovereign Being: His
charming beauty, His eternal love for us and all the benefits which He has bestowed upon us, His most unde-
serving and ungrateful creatures—all of which, alas,
make no impression on us without serious consideration!
All things that are round about us—the heavens, the
earth and every creature therein—cease not to preach
God to us and invite us to love Him. But without consideration, we are deaf to the voice of this whole creation; we
are like those that have eyes and see not, that have ears
and hear not. (Cf. *Mark* 8:18). Ah, the great and dreadful
mischiefs that follow from the absence of that true
knowledge of God which is the fruit of daily consideration! Is it not for this reason that the whole world is over-
run with wickedness and that Hell opens wide its jaws,
devouring without end or number the unhappy children
of Adam, because God is forgotten, because *"there is no
knowledge of God in the land"? (Osee* 4:1).

Consider thirdly that, to save our souls, we must also
know ourselves: We must know our misery and our corruption, that we may be humble and not trust in ourselves; we must know our irregular inclinations and
passions, that we may fight against them and overcome
them; we must study and watch the motions of our own
hearts, that we may not be surprised by sin and sleep in
death. And how can this all-necessary knowledge of ourselves, this "science of the Saints," be acquired without
the help of daily consideration? Ah, how unhappy are
they who know all other things and are strangers to
themselves! Let us then daily pray with St. Augustine,
Noverim te, Domine, noverim me.—"O Lord, give me
grace to know Thee; O Lord, give me grace to know
myself." [literally, "May I know Thee, O Lord; may I know
myself."] And let us labor for these two most necessary
kinds of knowledge by frequent consideration.

Consider fourthly that, in order to nourish in our souls
the wholesome fear of God, which is the beginning of true

wisdom, and to spur ourselves on in the way of virtue, we must also seriously reflect on the enormity of sin and the hatred which God bears to it; on the dreadful effect of sin in the soul and on the multitude of our own sins in particular; on the vanity, misery and deceitfulness of the world; on the comfort and happiness that accompany a virtuous life; on the shortness of time and the dreadful length of a miserable eternity; on the certainty and uncertainty of death and the sentiments which we shall have when we come to die; on the small number of the elect [those who are saved], etc., etc. Ah, Christians, let us not neglect this great means of salvation! It is the consideration of these truths that has made so many Saints, that has so often reclaimed even the most abandoned sinners. Oh, what a profound lethargy must that soul be in which is not aroused at the thunder of those dreadful truths—Death, Judgment, Hell, Eternity!

Consider fifthly the bitter but fruitless repentance of the damned, condemning their past folly in having thought so little about those things on which they shall now think for all eternity! [Then shall the damned say to themselves:] "Senseless wretches that we were; we had once our time, when, by thinking upon this miserable eternity, we might have escaped it. Those endless joys of Heaven were offered us at a cheap price, when a little reflection on them might have put us in the way of securing to ourselves the everlasting possession of them. But alas, we would not think then, and now it is too late!" O my Soul, learn thou by their misfortune to be wise! Reflect in this thy day on the things that pertain to thine eternal peace. Think well on thy last end. Meditate on the great truths of the Gospel. Thou must think of them either now or hereafter—when the thought of them will only serve to aggravate thy misery for all eternity.

Chapter 2

On the End or Purpose Of Our Creation

The Second Day

CONSIDER FIRST, O Christian Soul, that so many years ago thou wert not yet come into the world and that thy being was a mere nothing. The world had lasted nearly six thousand years, with innumerable transactions and revolutions in every nation, and where wast thou all that while? Alas, thou wast engulfed in the deep abyss of nothingness, infinitely beneath the condition of the meanest creature upon the earth! And what couldst thou do, remaining there? Learn, then, to humble thyself, whatever advantages thou mayest enjoy of nature or grace, since of thyself thou art nothing and all that thou hast above nothing has been given or loaned thee by thy Maker. Ah, poor Wretch, what hast thou to be proud of? Or what canst thou call thy own, but nothingness and sin, which is worse than nothingness?

Consider secondly that the Almighty Hand of God, descending into that deep abyss of nothingness, has drawn thee forth from thence and given thee this being which thou dost now enjoy, the most accomplished and perfect of any in this visible world, capable of knowing and loving God in this life and designed for an everlasting happiness with Him in the next. Admire and adore

4

the bounty of thy God, who from all eternity has designed this being for thee, preferable to so many millions of others which He has left behind, that had as much right to being as thou didst have. Look forward into that immense eternity for which thou hast been created and thankfully acknowledge that the love thy God bears to thee has neither beginning nor end, but reaches from eternity to eternity.

Consider thirdly that, having been created by Almighty God and having received thy whole being from Him, thou dost belong to Him by the justest of all rights and art obliged to consecrate to His service all thy powers, faculties and senses and that thou art guilty of a most crying injustice as often as thou dost abuse any part of thy being by employing it in the pursuit of vanity and sin. Ah, my Poor Soul, how little have we hitherto thought of this! How small a part of our thoughts, words and deeds has been referred to Him who is our First Beginning and therefore ought to be the Last End of all our actions! Be confounded at so great an abuse. Repent and amend!

Consider fourthly that God, who gave thee thy being and who created all other things in this visible world for thy service, has created thee for Himself alone. Not that He stood in need of thee or can receive from thee any increase or addition to His happiness, but that He might give thee His grace in this life and the endless joys of His kingdom in the next. Stand astonished, Christian Soul, at the bounty of thy Creator in making thee for so noble an End; and since thou wast made for God, be ashamed to content thyself with anything less than God. Learn, then, to show contempt for all that is earthly and temporal, as beneath thee and unworthy of thy affection. Lament over thy past folly and that of the far greater part of mankind, who spend their days in vain amusements, in restless cares about painted toys and mere trifles and seldom or never think of that Great End for which alone they came into this world.

Consider fifthly that all the powers and faculties of thy soul—thy will, thy memory, thine understanding and all the senses and parts of thy body—were all given thee by thy Creator as so many means to attain to this End of thy creation, to be employed during thy short abode in this transitory life in the service of thy God, and so to bring thee to the eternal enjoyment of Him in the sweet repose of His blessed kingdom. Alas, my Soul, have we not perverted all these gifts of our Maker in turning them all against the Giver? Have mercy on us, O Lord, have mercy on us; pardon our past treasons and give us grace now to begin to be wise for eternity.

Chapter 3

On the Benefits of God

The Third Day

CONSIDER FIRST, my Soul, how many and how great are thine obligations to the bounty of thy God. He has thought of thee from all eternity; He has loved thee from all eternity; all those blessings and favors which He has bestowed upon thee in time He designed for thee from all eternity; they are all the consequences of His eternal love for thee. Is it possible that so great a God, the Most High and the Most Holy, who dwells in eternity, should have set His affections upon such a poor sinful worm of the earth? Is it possible, my Soul, that thou shouldst have had a place from all eternity in the heart of thy God and that this Eternal Mind should never have been one moment without thinking of thee! Ah, poor Wretch! What return hast thou made for this Ancient Love? How late hast thou loved Him who has loved thee from all eternity! How little hast thou thought of Him who always thinks of thee!

Consider secondly that thy God has not only given thee, by creation, thy soul and body with all their powers and faculties—and in a word, whatever thou hast and whatever thou art—but He also preserves them in existence each moment and at all times by the benefit of conservation, which may be called a continual creation. For as nothing but His Almighty Hand could have given thee

7

this being that thou hast, so none but He could preserve thee from falling back into thy former nothingness— which must infallibly have happened to thee if thy God had but for one moment withdrawn His Supporting Hand. Poor Sinner, why didst thou not think of this when by thy repeated crimes thou wast waging war with thy God and He, with incomparable love, was night and day watching over thee? How didst thou dare presume—so often and for so long a time—to provoke Him who holds the thread of thy life in His hand and who at any moment could have crushed thee into nothingness, or cast thee headlong into Hell? Oh, blessed by all creatures be His Mercy forever for having borne with thee so long!

Consider thirdly the inestimable benefit of our Redemption, by which our loving God has rescued us from sin and from Hell, the just reward of sin. Alas, my Poor Soul, we must have been lost forever, had not this Sovereign Maker and Lord of Heaven and Earth loved us to that degree as to deliver Himself up to the most cruel and ignominious death of the Cross for our Redemption! *"Greater love than this no man hath, that a man lay down his life for his friends."* (*John* 15:13). But, O Dear Lord, Thou hast carried Thy love much further than this in dying for those who, by sin, were Thy declared enemies— in dying for such ungrateful wretches as would scarcely ever thank Thee for Thy love and seldom or never so much as pity Thy sufferings or take any notice of them! Ah, Christians, what shall we wonder at more: to see this Great Monarch of Heaven and Earth—in comparison with whom the whole creation is just nothing, or rather, less than nothing—expiring on a cross for such despica- ble worms as we are; or to see those who believe this amazing truth take so little notice of this immense love which will be a just subject of astonishment to men and Angels for all eternity?

Consider fourthly how much we owe to God for having called us to the True Faith, for having preferred us to so many millions whom He has left behind in darkness and in the shadow of death. Alas, poor souls, how deplorable is their condition, void as they are of the knowledge of Jesus Christ or of His only Spouse, the true Catholic Church! How little do they think of God or of the life to come! With how little apprehension or remorse do they run on from sin to sin and die impenitent! Ah, the goodness of God that has not allowed us to fall into such misery, though we were born and bred amidst a people seduced by error! Or if we have also had the misfortune, like our neighbors, to have gone astray from the womb [cf. *Psalm* 57:4], He has, by a more distinguished mercy, drawn us out of the dragon's jaws and brought us to His fold, the Catholic Church! Blessed be Our God forever for all His mercies! Oh, what an inestimable happiness it is to have, by the means of this grace of vocation, God Himself for our Father and His Holy Church for Our Mother, to pass this transitory life in the happy society of the only Spouse of God's only Son, to be daily partakers of the Sacraments (those heavenly conduits of divine grace), to live and die in the Communion of the Saints, etc.! Ah, *"Happy is that people whose God is the Lord!"* (*Psalm* 143:15).

Consider fifthly, O Christian Soul, whoever thou art, the particular providence of God toward thee! With how many graces He has protected thee in advance from thy tender years, from how many misfortunes He has preserved thee! Has He not borne with thee for a long time, while others have been cut off in their sins? Are there not millions now burning in Hell for lesser sins than thou hast committed? Reflect on the advantages which thou hast received above thousands of others: what conveniences of life, what friends, what health, etc., while so many—more worthy than thyself—have been abandoned to poverty and misery! Ah, wonder at the unspeakable goodness of thy God to thee! Be astonished and confounded at thy past ingratitude! Resolve henceforth never to cease giving Him thanks and blessing His Holy Name.

Chapter 4

On the Dignity and Obligations Of a Christian

The Fourth Day

CONSIDER FIRST that every Christian, by nature and inasmuch as he is a man, is the most perfect of all visible creatures, endowed with understanding and reason, composed of a body, whose structure is admirable, and of a spiritual and immortal soul, created to the image and likeness of God and capable of the eternal enjoyment of Him, enriched with a free will and advanced by his Creator to the dignity of lord and master of all other creatures—though not designed to meet with his happiness in any of them, but in the Creator alone. Ah, my Soul, hast thou hitherto been aware of the dignity of thy nature? Hast thou not too often, like the brute beasts, looked no further than this earth, that is, these present material and sensible things? Hast thou not too often made thyself a slave to creatures, which were only made to serve thee?

Consider secondly that every Christian, by Sanctifying Grace and inasmuch as he is a Christian, has been by the Sacrament of Baptism advanced to participation in the Divine Nature and has been made the adopted child of God, heir of God and co-heir with Christ! He has been made the temple of the Most High, consecrated by the

10

sprinkling of the blood of Christ and the unction of His grace, and has received at the same time an unquestionable right and title to an everlasting kingdom! O Christian Soul, didst thou ever yet entertain a serious thought of the greatness of this dignity to which thou wast raised at thy Baptism?* How has thy life corresponded with this dignity? O Child of Heaven, how long wilt thou be a slave to the earth?

Consider thirdly that, as the dignity of a Christian is very great, so also are the obligations that attend this dignity greater than the generality of Christians imagine! These obligations are, in short, comprised in our baptismal promises. The first condition, upon which we were, by Baptism, adopted into God's family, was that of *faith*. The minister of Christ examined us at the font upon every article of our belief, and to each interrogation we answered by the mouths of our godfathers and godmothers, *Credo,* "I do believe." What has thy faith been, O my Soul? Has it been conformable to this thy profession? Has it been firm, without wavering? Has it been generous, so as not to be ashamed of the doctrine of thy heavenly Master or of the maxims of His Gospel? Has it shown itself in thy actions? Or hast thou been of the number of those whose life gives the lie to their faith—of whom the Apostle complains that they *"profess that they know God, but in their works they deny him." (Titus* 1:16).

Consider fourthly that at our Baptism we made a solemn renunciation of "the devil, and all his works and all his pomps." Have we ever seriously reflected upon this renunciation? Or do we rightly understand the obligations of it? And yet our title to the inheritance of our heavenly Father is forfeited the moment that we are false to this sacred commitment by commiting mortal

---

*For a whole book on all the marvelous effects of the Sanctifying Grace that we receive at Baptism, read the Catholic classic, *The Glories of Divine Grace*, by Fr. Matthias Scheeben (1835-1888); TAN, 2000. —*Publisher*, 2006.

sin. Ah, my Soul, if thou hast renounced Satan, take care that in the practice of thy life thou keep far from him; take care that thou be no longer his slave by sin. Fly from all his works, the works of darkness! Let him henceforth find nothing in thee that he may claim for his own and by means of which he may also lay claim to thee. Despise his vain pomps, the false appearances of worldly grandeur, the prodigality, vanity and sinful entertainments by which he cheats poor worldlings into his nets. And if at any time thou art invited to take part in these fooleries, repeat to thyself those words of St. Augustine: "What hast thou to do with the pomps of the devil, which thou has renounced?"

Consider fifthly that at Baptism each one of us, according to the ancient ceremony of the Catholic Church, was clothed with a white garment, which the minister of Christ gave us with these words: *"Receive this white garment, which thou shalt carry without spot or stain before the judgment seat of Christ."* Happy souls that comply with this obligation! What a comfort will it be to them in life, what a joy and satisfaction in death to have kept this robe of innocence undefiled! But O Baptismal Innocence, where shall we find thee in this unhappy age? O Blindness and Stupidity of the children of Adam, who part so easily with such an inestimable treasure! Alas, my Poor Soul, has this not been thy misfortune? Oh make haste to wash away with penitential tears those dreadful stains of sin, which otherwise must be the eternal fuel of Hell's merciless flames!

Chapter 5

On the Vanity of the World

The Fifth Day

CONSIDER FIRST those words of the wisest of men: *"Vanity of vanities, and all is vanity."* (*Ecclesiastes* 1:2). And reflect how truly vain are all those things, which deluded worldlings seek with so much eagerness. Honors, riches and worldly pleasures are all but painted bubbles, which look at a distance as if they were something, but have nothing of real substance in them, and instead of a solid content and joy, bring nothing with them but a trifling satisfaction of a moment, followed with cares, uneasiness, apprehensions and remorse. Ah, bubbles indeed, which their admirers no sooner offer to lay hold on, but they dissolve into air and leave their hands empty! Oh, how justly were all worldly enjoyments likened to a dream by the Royal Prophet: *Dormierunt somnum suum, et nihil invenerunt omnes viri divitiarum in manibus suis.—"They have slept their sleep, and all the men of riches have found nothing in their hands."* (*Psalm* 75:6). *"O ye sons of men, how long will you be dull of heart? Why do you love vanity and seek after lying?"* (*Psalm* 4:3).

Consider secondly that saying of St. Augustine, "Thou hast made us for Thyself, O Lord, and our hearts are restless until they rest in Thee." (*Confessions,* Bk. 1, Ch. 1). And reflect, that our Great Creator has given us a noble soul, made to His own image and like Him, spiritual and immortal, which therefore can never find its happiness in earthly or fading things! No, my Soul, thou hast an understanding and a will, capable of contemplating the Sovereign Beauty and Sovereign Truth and of enjoying the one Supreme Infinite Good, and whatever is less than He is not worthy of thee. Ah, resolve then no longer to tire thyself and waste away thy spirits in running like a child after these butterflies. But since thou canst not be without seeking for happiness, seek it in God's name, where it is to be found, that is, in the way of virtue and devotion, and not in the by-paths, which lead to endless misery!

Consider thirdly the shortness of all worldly enjoyments. Man's days are very short: the longest life is less than one moment if compared to eternity. *"For a thousand years in thy sight are as yesterday, which is past."* (*Psalm* 89:4). That is the very truth! Alas! Does not daily experience show us that we are here today and gone tomorrow—and no sooner are we out of sight, but out of mind also? For as soon as we are in the grave, those whom we leave behind think no more of us. *"All flesh is grass,"* says the Prophet Isaias, *"and all the glory thereof as the flower of the field."* (*Isaias* 40:6). And what is that but flourishing in the morning and fading in the evening? Oh, how truly is our life likened by St. James to a vapor, or a thin smoke, which is dispersed by the first puff of wind, and we see no more of it! (Cf. *James* 4:15). How justly is it compared by Solomon to a shadow, or to the passing of a bird upon the wing, or to an arrow from the bow, which leaves no mark in the air behind it! (*Wisdom* 5:9, 11-12). Ah, how vain it is to set our hearts upon what we must so soon leave!

Consider fourthly what is now become of all those great ones of this world, those mighty monarchs, those gallant generals, those wise statesman, those celebrated beauties, etc., who made such a figure a hundred years ago? Alas, they are all long since dead and gone! And now few, or none, ever thinks of them or scarce knows there ever were any such persons. Just so will it be with us a few years hence. Ah, Worldlings, give ear for one moment to those who are gone before you, who from their silent monuments where the remainder of their dust lies mingled with the common earth, call upon you in the words of the Wise Man, *Memento judicii mei, sic enim erit et tuum: mihi heri, tibi hodie—"Remember my judgment, for thine also shall be so: yesterday for me, and today for thee."* (*Ecclesiasticus* 38:23). "Remember what we are come to; it will soon be the same with you. It was our turn yesterday; it will be yours today. We once had our parts to act upon the stage of the world; we once were young, strong and healthy, as you are now, and thought as little as you do of what we are now come to. Like you, we set our hearts upon those trifles and toys that we could enjoy but for a moment, and for these we neglected eternity. Senseless wretches as we were, we chose to be slaves to a cheating world, to inconstant perishable creatures, which abandoned us so soon, rather than to serve that Lord and Master to whom nothing dies and who—neither in life nor in death—ever forsakes those that forsake not him."

O Christians, let us take this warning: Let the miscarriages of so many others teach us to be wise; let us not set our hearts on this miserable world or look upon anything as truly great but that which is eternal!

Chapter 6

On the Happiness of Serving God

The Sixth Day

CONSIDER FIRST those words of the Prophet Isaias, *"Say to the just man, It is well,"* (*Isaias* 3:10), and reflect on the manifold advantages which this short word *"well"* comprises and ensures to the just, both for time and eternity. Honors, riches and pleasures are the things on which the world sets the greatest value. But they are not to be found where the world seeks them, but only in the service of God. Can any honor upon earth be comparable to that of being a servant, a friend, an adopted son of the great King of Heaven? Such a soul is far more dignified in the eyes of God and His Angels than the greatest emperor in the universe. She is a child of the eternal Father, a spouse of the eternal Son, a temple of the eternal Spirit, heiress of the Kingdom of Heaven, and sister and companion to the Angels. O my Soul, let such honors as these be the only objects of thy ambition.

Consider secondly that the truest riches are to be found in the service of God, not indeed those worldly possessions, which are accompanied by so many cares and fears, are exposed to so many accidents, and which are not capable of satisfying the heart; but the inestimable treasure of the grace of God, which is the seed of everlasting glory; the gifts of the Holy Ghost; the love of God;

in a word, God Himself, whom the whole world cannot take from the soul, unless she be so miserably blind as to drive Him away by mortal sin. Add to this the fatherly providence of God over the just; that His eyes are always upon them, to take care of their welfare; that His Angels always encamp about them, to guard them by night and by day (Cf. *Psalm* 33:8); that as He formerly said to Abraham, *"Fear not . . . I am thy protector and thy reward exceeding great."* (*Genesis* 15:1). He is their friend, and the best of friends; the Shepherd of their souls, who leads them out to His admirable pastures, to the fountains of living water. His tenderness toward them is beyond that of a father, nay, beyond that of the tenderest mother. (Cf. *Isaias* 49:15-16). In short, God is all things to those who fear Him. O my Soul, seek no other treasure than Him. Fear nothing but losing Him. If thou have Him, nothing can make thee miserable; but without Him, nothing can make thee happy!

Consider thirdly the pleasures that accompany a virtuous life: the satisfaction, peace and joy of a good conscience, which by the Wise Man is likened to a continual banquet; the consolations of the Holy Ghost; the comfortable expectation of a happy eternity after our exit out of this vale of tears; a holy confidence in the protection and providence of God; and a perfect conformity in all things to His blessed will. From these fountains flow such delights as cannot be conceived by worldlings, who have no experience of them: pleasures pure and spiritual, which sweeten all the crosses of this life, which are an unspeakable comfort in death, and which carry with them a certain foretaste of the immortal joys of Heaven. Whereas all worldly pleasures, like the world itself, are false and deceitful, always besprinkled with something of bitterness, and accompanied by uneasiness, and followed with remorse, and end at last in eternal sorrow.

Consider fourthly that saying of our Saviour, *"But one thing is necessary."* (*Luke* 10:42). And what is that one thing, O my Soul, which alone can make thee happy, both here and hereafter? It is to serve thy God and to provide in earnest for eternity. All time, compared to eternity, is less than nothing: so are all temporal concerns, if compared to the concern of eternity. This in reality is thy only business. If thou take care of this, all is well; if thou neglect this, all is lost, and lost forever! As for all other things of which thou mayest stand in need in this life, give ear again to the same Saviour, *"Seek ye therefore first the kingdom of God, and his justice, and all these things shall be added unto you."* (*Matthew* 6:33). Conclude then, my Soul, since thy welfare, both temporal and eternal, depends on serving God, to make this, for the future, thy only care. Thus only shalt thou meet true comfort here; thus only shalt thou come to never-ending happiness hereafter.

Chapter 7

On Death

The Seventh Day

CONSIDER FIRST that there is nothing more certain than death. *"It is appointed unto men once to die, and after this the judgment."* (*Hebrews* 9:27). The sentence is general; it is pronounced upon all the children of Adam. Neither wealth, nor strength, nor wisdom, nor all the power of this world can exempt anyone from this common doom. From the first moment of our birth, we are hastening to our death; every moment brings it nearer to us. The day will come—it will most certainly come, and only God knows how soon—when we shall never see the night. Or the night will come when we shall never see the morning. The time will most certainly come when thou, my Soul, must bid a long farewell to this cheating world and to all that thou hast admired therein—and even to thy own body, the individual companion of thy life—and take thy journey to another country, where all that thou settest a value upon here will appear as smoke. Learn, then, to despise this miserable world and all its enjoyments, with which thou must part so soon, whether thou willest to or no.

Consider secondly that, as nothing is more certain and inevitable than death, so nothing is more uncertain than the time, the place, the manner and all other circumstances of our death. "O my Soul," says St. Francis de

Sales, "thou must one day part with this body, but when shall that day be? Shall it be in winter, or in summer? In the city, or in the country? By day, or by night? Shall it be suddenly, or on notice given thee? Shalt thou have leisure to make thy Confession? Shalt thou have the assistance of thy spiritual father? Alas, of all this, thou knowest nothing at all! Only certain it is that thou must die and that, as it almost always happens, much sooner than thou dost imagine."

Consider thirdly that death, being so certain and the time or manner of it so uncertain, it would be no small comfort if a man could die more than once, that so, if he should have the misfortune once to die ill, he might repair the fault by taking more care a second time. But alas! We can die but once, and when once we have set our foot within the gates of eternity, there is no coming back. If we die once well, it will be always well; but if once ill, it will be ill for all eternity. O Dreadful Moment, upon which depends an endless eternity! O blessed Lord, prepare us for that fatal hour!

Consider fourthly the folly and stupidity of the greatest part of men, who though they daily see some or other of their friends, acquaintances or neighbors carried off by death—and that very often in the vigor of their youth, very often by sudden death—yet always imagine death to be at a distance from them, as if those arrows of death which are falling on all sides of them would not in their turn reach them too; or as if they had a greater security than so many others, who are daily swept away. Senseless Worldlings! Why will you not open your eyes? Why will you fondly imagine yourselves secure from the stroke of death, when you cannot even promise yourselves so much as one single day of life? How many will die before the end of this month that are as young, as strong and as healthy as you are? Who knows but you may be of that number? Ah, Christians, take care lest you be surprised! Set your house in order; and for the future, fly from sin, the only evil, which makes death terrible.

Live always in those dispositions in which you would gladly be found at the hour of your death. To act otherwise is to renounce both religion and reason.

Consider fifthly the state and condition of this corruptible body of ours as soon as we are dead. Alas, it immediately becomes pale, stiff, loathsome and hideous, insomuch that our dearest friends can scarcely endure to watch one night in the same room with it, much less bear to lie in the same bed! And so fast does it tend to stench and corruption that its nearest relations are the first to desire to get it out of the house and to lay it deep under ground, that it may not infect the air. But what companions, what attendants must it meet with there? Worms and maggots. For these, O Man, thou art pampering thy body! These are to be thine inheritance—or rather, they are to inherit thee. Whatever thou art today, tomorrow thou art to be the food of worms. Ah, Worldlings, who are enamoured with your own and others' beauty, and thereby too often drawn from your allegiance to God, vouchsafe for once to reflect upon the condition to which both you and they must soon be reduced, and you will see what little reason you have to set your affections upon these painted dunghills, which will so quickly betray what they are and end in stench and corruption. We read that St. Francis Borgia was so touched with the bare sight of the ghastly countenance of the Empress Isabella after death, whom he had seen a little before in all her majesty and all her charms, as to conceive an eternal disgust of this world and a happy resolution of consecrating himself wholly to the service of that King who never dies. Let similar considerations move us to a similar resolution.

Chapter 8

On the Sentiments That We Shall Have at the Hour of Our Death

The Eighth Day

CONSIDER FIRST, O Christian Soul, what will be thy sentiments at the hour of death with regard to this world and all its perishable goods, vain honors, false riches and cheating pleasures. Alas! The world must then end in thy regard! It will turn upside down before thine eyes, and thou wilt begin to see the nothingness of all those things on which thou hast here set thy heart. How wilt thou then despise all worldly honors and preferments when thou seest thyself at the brink of the grave, where the worm will make no distinction between the king and the beggar! How little account wilt thou then make of the esteem of men, who then will think no more of thee! How wilt thou undervalue thy riches, which must now be left behind thee, when six feet of earth and a coffin and a shroud will be all thy possession! How despicable will all worldly pleasures seem to thee, which at the best could never give thee any true satisfaction, and now fly from thee and dissolve into smoke in thy sight! Ah, my Poor Soul, enter now into the same sentiments which thou shalt certainly have at the hour of thy death! Thus, and only thus, thou shalt be out of danger of being imposed upon by this deceitful world.

Consider secondly what will then be thy thoughts with regard to thy sins, when that curtain will begin to be withdrawn with which thy busy self-love has industriously hidden or disguised the deformity and malice of thy crimes and they shall be set before thine eyes in their true light; when so many things which thou wast willing to persuade thyself were but small faults, or none at all, will present themselves before thee in other colors as great and hideous offenses; when the false conscience which thou hast framed to thyself and under the cover of which thou hast passed over many things in thy Confessions as slight and inconsiderable—which thou wast ashamed to declare or unwilling to forsake—shall no longer be able to maintain itself at the approach of death. Ah, what anguish, what confusion, what dreadful temptations to despair must such a sight as this give to the dying sinner! Learn thou, my Soul, to take better measures now in time, and thus to prevent so great a misery.

Consider thirdly and take a closer look at the lamentable state of a sinner at the hour of his death, when all things seem to conspire against him and whichsoever way he looks for any ease or comfort, he can find none. Before his eyes he sees a whole army of sins mustered up, a viper's brood of his own offspring, which stick close to him and, assailing him with their united forces, make him already begin to feel the complaints of that never-dying worm of conscience, which shall be the eternal torment of the damned. Oh, how gladly would he shake off this troublesome company! But all in vain; they are resolved not to leave him. If he looks back into his past life to seek for some good works to oppose to this army of sins, alas, he finds the good that he has done has been so inconsiderable, so insignificant, as to afford him no hope of its weighing down the scales when balanced with his multiplied crimes. His very prayers, the Confessions and Communions which he has made, fly now in his face and upbraid him with his wretched negligence and his sacrilegious abuse of these great means of salvation. The sight of all things about him—his wife, his children, his friends, his worldly goods, which he has loved more than his God—serve for nothing now but to increase his anguish. And what is his greatest misery is that the agonies of his sickness give him little or no leisure or ability to apply himself seriously to the greatest and most difficult of all concerns, which is a perfect conversion to God after a long habit of sin. Oh how truly may the sinner now repeat those words of the Psalmist, *"The sorrows of death have compassed me, and the perils of hell have found me!"* (*Psalm* 114:3). Oh what unspeakable anguish must it be to see himself just embarking upon eternity— an infinite and endless duration, an immense ocean, to whose farther shore the poor sailor can never reach—and to have so much reason to fear that it will be to him an eternity of woe!

Consider fourthly, my Soul, what thy sentiments will be at the hour of thy death with relation to the service of God, to virtue and to devotion. How lovely then will the way of virtue appear to thee! How wilt thou then wish to have followed that charming path! Oh what a satisfaction is it to a dying man to have lived well! What a comfort to see himself now at the end of all his labors and dangers, to find himself at the gates of eternal rest, of everlasting peace, after a long and doubtful war! He may now come down securely from his watch-tower and repose himself forever in the kingdom of his Father. Oh what a pleasure, what a joy, to look forward into that blessed eternity! Oh how *"precious in the sight of the Lord is the death of his saints!"* (*Psalm* 115:15). Ah, *"Let my soul die the death of the just, and my last end be like to them!"* (*Numbers* 23:10). Christians, if we would die the death of the just, we must live the life of the just! The only security for a good death is a good life.

Consider fifthly, or rather, conclude from the foregoing considerations on death to make it the whole business of your life to prepare for death. Upon dying well depends nothing less than eternity. If we die badly, we are lost, and lost forever! As then we came into the world for nothing else but to provide for eternity, so we may truly say that we came into the world for nothing else but to learn to die well. This is the great lesson which we must all study. Alas, if we miss it when we are called to the test, endless woe must of necessity be the consequence! Ah, how hard it is to learn to perform well that which can be done but once!

Chapter 9

On the Particular Judgment After Death

The Ninth Day

CONSIDER FIRST that the soul is no sooner parted from the body than she is immediately presented before the Judge in order to give an account of her whole life, of all that she has thought, said or done during her abode in the body, and to receive sentence accordingly. For the truth that the eternal fate of every soul is decided by a Particular Judgment immediately after death is what we learn from the Gospel in the example of Dives and Lazarus. And the sentence that passes here will be ratified in the General Judgment at the Last Day. Christians, how stand your accounts with God? What could you be able to say for yourselves if this night you should be cited to the bar? This may perhaps be your case. Remember that your Lord will come when you least expect Him. Take care, then, always to be ready.

Consider secondly how exact, how rigorous this judgment will be, in which even the least idle word cannot escape the scrutiny of the Judge. Oh, what treasures of iniquity will here come to light when the veil shall be removed which hides at present the greatest part of our sins from the eyes of the world, and even from our own, and the whole history of our lives shall at once be exposed to our view! Good God! who can be able to bear this dreadful sight? Here shall the poor soul be brought to a most exact examination of all that she has done, or left undone, in the whole time of her pilgrimage in this mortal body: how she has corresponded with the divine inspirations; what use she has made of God's graces; what profit she has reaped from the Sacraments which she has received, from the Word of God which she has heard or read; what advantage she has made of those favorable circumstances in which God Almighty has placed her; how she has employed the talents with which He has entrusted her. Even her best works shall be carefully sifted: her prayers, her fasts, her almsdeeds, the intention with which she has undertaken them, the manner in which she has performed them; all shall be weighed, not in the deceitful balance of the judgment of men, but in the scales of the eternal sanctuary. Ah, how many of our actions will here be found to lack weight, according to that saying of Daniel, *"Thou art weighed in the balance, and art found wanting."* (*Daniel* 5:27). O Lord, *"Enter not into judgment with thy servant,"* O Lord, *"for in thy sight no man living shall be justified."* (*Psalm* 142:2).

Consider thirdly the qualities of the Judge before whom we must appear. He is infinitely wise, and therefore cannot be deceived; He is infinitely powerful, and therefore cannot be withstood; He is infinitely just, and therefore He will render to everyone according to his works. (Cf. *Apocalypse* 2:23). No favor is to be expected at this day; the time of merit and of acceptable repentance is now at an end. Ah, Christians, **think well on it** now, while it is your day! You may *now* wash away your sins by penitential tears and thus hide them from the eyes of your Future Judge; you may *at present* tie up His hands by humble prayer; you may *now* appeal from His justice to the court of His mercy and cause Him to cancel the sentence that stands against you! But on that day, you will find Him inexorable! Your prayers and tears will then come too late.

Consider fourthly the inestimable comfort that the souls of the just shall receive at this day from the company of their good works, which like an invincible rampart shall surround them on all sides and keep their hellish foes at a distance. O my Soul, let us take care to provide ourselves with such attendants as these against that hour which is to decide our eternal fate. These are friends indeed that will not forsake us, even in death, and will effectually plead our cause at the bar, where no other eloquence will be regarded.

Consider fifthly in what a wretched plight the sinner who has taken no care to lay up any such provision of good works shall now stand before his Judge. Oh, how all things speak to him the melancholy sentence that is just now going to fall upon his guilty head! Whatever way he looks, he sees nothing that can give him any comfort, but on the contrary, all things that contribute to his greater anguish and terror. Beneath his feet he sees Hell open, ready to swallow him up; above his head an angry Judge preparing to thunder out against him the irrevocable sentence of damnation; on his right hand he sees his Guardian Angel, now abandoning him; on his left the devils, his merciless enemies, just ready to seize upon him and only waiting for the bidding of the Judge. If he look behind him, he discovers a cheating world, which now retires from him; if he look before him, he meets with nothing but a dismal eternity. Within him he feels the intolerable stings of a guilty conscience; and on all sides of him he perceives an army of hideous monsters, his own sins, more terrible to him now than the furies of Hell. Good God, deliver me from ever having any share in such a scene of misery!

Consider sixthly that, in order to prevent the judgment of God from falling heavily upon us after our death, we must take care now, during our life, to judge and chastise ourselves by doing serious penance for our sins. Thus, and only thus, shall we disarm the justice of God enkindled by our sins. Let us follow the advice of Him who is to be our Judge, who calls upon us to watch and pray at all times, that so we may be found worthy to escape these dreadful dangers and stand with confidence before the Son of man. (Cf. *Luke* 21:36). Ah, let this Judgment be always before our eyes! Let us daily meditate on this account that we are one day to give. Let us never forget that there is an eye above that sees all things; that there is an ear that hears all things; that there is a hand that writes down all our thoughts, words and deeds in the great accounting book; that all our actions pass from our hands to the hands of God; and that what is done in time passes not away with time, but shall subsist after all time is past. *"O that they would be wise and would understand, and would provide for their last end!"* (*Deuteronomy* 32:29).

Chapter 10

On the Great Accounting Day

The Tenth Day

CONSIDER FIRST that nothing can be conceived more terrible than the prospect which the Scripture gives us of the Last Accounting Day, with all the prodigies that shall go before it: the sun darkened, the moon red as blood, the stars without light and seeming to fall from the firmament, the earth shaken with violent earthquakes, the sea swelling and roaring with unusual tempests, the elements all in confusion, and all of nature in disorder. *"The day of the Lord,"* says the prophet Joel, is *"a day of darkness and of gloominess, a day of clouds and whirlwinds. . . . Before the face thereof a devouring fire, and behind it a burning flame. . . . At their presence the earth hath trembled, the heavens are moved; the sun and moon are darkened, and the stars have withdrawn their shining."* (*Joel* 2:1, 2, 3, 10). And the prophet Sophonias cries out, *"That day is a day of wrath, a day of tribulation and distress, a day of calamity and misery, a day of darkness and obscurity, a day of clouds and whirlwinds."* (*Sophonias* 1:15). Can anything be more frightful than these descriptions? Ah, what will then be the thoughts of sinful man, who sees himself threatened by all these signs? Alas! He shall perfectly wither away with fear in expectation of that tragedy which must follow these dreadful preludes.

Consider secondly that, the Last Day being come, fire raging like an impetuous torrent shall, by the command of God, consume the whole surface of the earth and all that is thereon; nothing shall escape it. Where, O Worldlings, will then be all your stately palaces, your pleasant seats, your gardens, fountains and grottoes, your gold, silver and precious stones, etc. Alas, all that you have set your hearts on in this world shall in a moment be reduced to ashes, to show you the vanity of the things that you loved and your own folly in placing your affection upon such glittering shadows, upon such painted bubbles. Learn then, my Soul, to despise this world and all its goods, since all must end in ashes and smoke; and lay up for thyself a treasure in Heaven, which alone will be out of the reach of this last fire.

Consider thirdly that, the final end of this world being now come, the Archangel shall sound the last trumpet and raise his voice with a *Surgite mortui . . . "Arise ye dead and come to judgment"*: a voice that shall at once be heard over all the universe, that shall pierce the highest heavens and penetrate down to the lowest abyss of Hell. At this voice, in an instant, by God's almighty power, all the children of Adam, from the first to the last, shall arise from the dust; and every soul shall be again united to its respective body, nevermore to part for eternity. O my Soul, let this last trumpet echo always in thine ears. Oh, take care to prevent the terrors of this summons by hearkening now to another summons—that of the great trumpet of the Holy Ghost—who calls upon thee by the mouth of the Apostle, *"Rise, thou that sleepest, and arise from the dead,"* that is, from the death of sin, *"and Christ shall enlighten thee."* (*Ephesians* 5:14). It is thus by having part in the first Resurrection that thou shalt provide in time against that dreadful hour when *"time shall be no longer."* (*Apocalypse* 10:6). It is thus thou shalt escape the second death.

Consider fourthly the wonderful difference there will be at the time of this General Resurrection between the bodies of the just and those of the wicked. The just shall arise in bodies most beautiful, more pure than the stars, more resplendent than the sun, immortal and impassible. But the wicked shall arise in bodies suitable to their deserts—foul, black, hideous, and in every way loathsome and insupportable—immortal, it is true, but to no other end than to endure immortal torments! What an inexpressible rack will it be to these wretched souls, to be forced into such carcasses, to be condemned to an eternal confinement in so horrid and so filthy an abode! Ah, take thou care, my Soul, to keep thy body pure now from the corruption of carnal sins, lest otherwise it be one day an aggravation of thine eternal misery.

Consider fifthly with how much satisfaction and joy the souls of the just shall be united again to their bodies, which they have so long desired, with what affection they shall embrace those fellow partners of all their labors, of all their sufferings and mortifications, and now designed, by sharing in the glory of the heavenly Sion, to give an addition to their eternal happiness. But oh, what dreadful curses shall pass at the melancholy meeting of the souls and bodies of the reprobate! "Accursed Carcass," will the soul say, "was it to please thee, to indulge thy brutish inclinations that I have forfeited the immortal joys of Heaven? Ah, Wretch, to give thee a filthy pleasure for a moment, I have damned both myself and thee to all eternity. O thrice accursed Carrion, it is just that thou who hast been the cause of my damnation shouldst be my partner in eternal woe!" But rather, ought not *thou*, Unhappy Soul, to be a thousand times accursed by the body, since it was *thy* business and it was in *thy* power to have subjected its passions and lusts to the rule of reason and religion, and thou didst rather choose, for the sake of a momentary satisfaction, to enslave thyself to its sensual inclinations and so to purchase Hell for thyself and it. Ah, Christians, let us learn to be wise by the consideration of the misfortunes of others!

Chapter 11

On the General Judgment

The Eleventh Day

CONSIDER FIRST that the dead, being all risen, shall immediately be assembled together in the place designed for the Last Judgment, commonly believed to be the valley of Josaphat, near Jerusalem, in the sight of Mount Olivet and Mount Calvary, where Our Lord heretofore shed His blood for our redemption. What a sight will it be to behold here all the children of Adam, that innumerable multitude of all nations, ages and degrees, standing together without any distinction now of rich or poor, great or little, master or servant, monarch or subject—excepting only the distinction of good and bad, which shall be wonderful and eternal. Alas, how mean a figure will an Alexander or a Caesar make at this appearance—or any of those great heroes of antiquity, whose very names have made whole nations tremble! Those mighty monarchs who once had the world at their beck and call are now leveled with the meanest of their slaves and [if they are damned] would wish a thousand times never to have borne the sceptre or worn the diadem.

Consider secondly that, the dead being now assembled together, the Great Judge shall descend from Heaven with great glory and majesty, surrounded by all His heavenly courtiers and all the legions of Angels. Oh, how different from His first coming will be that of His second appearance! His first coming was in great meekness and humility, because that was *our* day, in which He came to redeem us by His mercy; but at His second coming, it will be *His* day, when He shall arm Himself with all the terrors of His justice, to revenge upon sinful man the cause of His injured mercy, with a final vengeance, once and for all. Miserable Sinners, how will you be able to stand His face or endure His wrathful countenance? Ah, then it is that you will begin to cry out to the mountains and rocks to fall upon you and hide you from the face of Him that sitteth on the throne and from the wrath of the Lamb! (Cf. *Apocalypse* 6:16). Nay, such a dread and terror will the very sight of this incensed Judge carry with it that you shall even wish a thousand times to hide your guilty heads in the lowest Hell rather than endure His dreadful appearance! But all in vain; you must endure it!

Consider thirdly that before the Judge shall be borne the royal standard of the Cross, shining more brightly than the sun, to the great comfort of the good and to the unspeakable anguish and confusion of the wicked for having made so little use of the inestimable benefit of their Redemption. Here they shall plainly see how much their God has suffered for their salvation, how great has been His love for them, that boundless and unparalleled love which brought Him down from the Throne of Glory and nailed Him to the Cross. Oh, how they will then condemn their own obstinacy in sin, their blindness and ingratitude! Oh, how this glorious ensign will justify in the face of the whole universe the conduct of God and the eternity of the torments of Hell, for what less than a miserable eternity can be punishment enough for so much obstinacy in evil after so much love.

Consider fourthly how, at the command of the Sovereign Judge, which shall be instantly obeyed, the servants of God shall be picked out from the midst of that vast multitude and placed with honor on His right hand; while the wicked, with all those evil spirits, whose part they have taken, shall with ignominy be driven to the left. Oh, dreadful and eternal separation, after which these two companies shall never again meet! And Thou, my Soul, where dost thou expect to stand at that day? In which of these two companies shalt thou be ranked? Thou hast it now in thy choice: choose then *now* that *"better part, which will never be taken away from thee."* (Cf. *Luke* 10:42). *Flee now from the midst of* Babylon (Cf. *Jeremias* 51:6); renounce *now* the false maxims, the corrupt customs, the sinful amusements of worldlings; separate thyself from the wicked *in time*, that thou mayest not be involved in their damnation *in eternity!*

Consider *fifthly* what will then be the thoughts of the great ones of this world: what fury, what envy, what bitter anguish and confusion will oppress their souls when they shall see the poor in spirit, the meek and humble—who were so contemptible in their eyes while they were here in this mortal life—now honored and exalted in the sight of the whole universe, and themselves treated with so much contempt! Hearken to their complaints, as they are set down by the Wise Man: *"These are they whom we had some time in derision and for a parable of reproach. We fools esteemed their life madness and their end without honour. Behold how they are numbered among the children of God, and their lot is among the saints."* (*Wisdom* 5:3-5). *Ergo erravimus a via veritatis.—"Therefore we have erred from the way of truth!"* (*Wisdom* 3:6). Alas! After all, we are the persons that have been mistaken, we that have unfortunately run on in the wrong way! And they were truly wise in making a better choice, which afforded them comfort in life and has now entitled them to endless joys.

Consider *sixthly* how much the anguish and humiliation of the wicked will be increased at the opening of the Books of Conscience, when all the guilt of their whole lives shall be laid open in the public view of the universe! Poor Sinner, what will thy thoughts be when those crimes which thou hast committed in the greatest secrecy and which thou wouldst not have had known for all the world, those abominations which thou didst imagine were covered with the obscurity of night and darkness and which thou didst flatter thyself that thy friends and acquaintances would never know, those works of iniquity which perhaps thou couldst not find in thy heart to reveal to even one person (tied by all laws to a perpetual secrecy) shall now all be exposed in their true colors to the eyes of the whole world, Angels and men, good and bad, to thine eternal shame! Ah! Christians, it is now in thy power to prevent by a sincere repentance and Confession this humiliation which thou must otherwise one day suffer.

Chapter 12

On the Last Sentence of the Good and Bad

The Twelfth Day

CONSIDER FIRST how this great trial shall be concluded by a final definitive sentence in favor of the just and for the condemnation of the wicked. And first, the Sovereign Judge, turning Himself toward His elect, with a most sweet and amiable countenance, shall invite them into His happy mansions of everlasting bliss: *"Come, ye blessed of my Father, possess you the kingdom prepared for you from the foundation of the world."* (*Matthew* 25:34). Oh, Happy Invitation! Happy, thrice happy they that shall be found worthy to hear that friendly sentence! What unspeakable satisfaction, what torrents of joy and pleasure will the hearing of it give to these blessed creatures! *"I rejoiced,"* says the Royal Prophet, *"at the things that were said to me; we shall go into the house of the Lord."* (*Psalm* 121:1). But oh what envy, what rage and malice will the reprobate feel at the hearing of this invitation, when they shall see several of their acquaintance called to take possession of that eternal kingdom which they might also have so easily purchased, but by their own folly and stupidity have blindly exchanged for the flames of Hell!

Consider secondly and ponder at leisure upon this

37

happy sentence: *"Come,"* says the Judge, *"ye blessed of my Father, . . . etc." "Come"* from the vale of tears, where, for a little while you have been tried and afflicted by the appointment of My Providence, to the Kingdom of never-ending joy, where grief and sorrow will be no more. Come from the place of banishment, where for a time you have sighed and groaned at a distance from your heavenly country, to your Everlasting Home, where you shall meet with all that your heart can desire to complete your happiness; where you shall be forever inebriated with the plenty of My house and drink forever at the fountain of life. Arise, My Beloved, the winter is now past, the floods and storms are over, arise and come. (Cf. *Cant. of Cants.* 2:10-13). Oh, universal and eternal blessing! How my poor soul scorns all other happiness in hopes of having a share one day in this blessed sentence!

Consider thirdly how the Great Judge, after having invited the just to His glorious kingdom, turning Himself towards the wicked on his left, with fire in His eyes and terror in His countenance, shall thunder out against them the dreadful sentence of their eternal doom in these words: *"Depart from me, ye cursed, into everlasting fire, which was prepared for the devil and his angels."* (*Matthew* 25:41). Christian Souls, weigh well every word of this dismal sentence! *"Depart"* forever *"from me"* and from the joys of My kingdom! Oh terrible excommunication! Oh cruel divorce! Oh eternal banishment! Who can express, who can conceive what it is to be forever separated from our God, our First Beginning and our Last End, our Great and Sovereign Good! Ah Wretches, who make so little now of losing your God by mortal sin, what will you think then, when you shall be sentenced to this eternal banishment from Him, doomed to seek Him for all eternity, and yet never to meet with Him in any of His attributes, except His avenging justice, the weight of which you shall feel forever? But take notice whither you are to go when you go from your God: Alas! *"into ever-lasting fire,"* there to lead an ever-dying life, there to endure a never-ending death, in the company of the devil and his angels, to whom you made yourselves slaves and who shall now, without control, exercise forever their tyranny over you.

Consider fourthly that dreadful and universal curse which this just but dismal sentence involves: *"Depart from me, ye cursed,"* says the Sovereign Judge, as if He were to say, "Go, depart from Me, but let My curse go with you. I would have given you My blessing, but you would not have it. A curse you chose, and a curse shall be your everlasting inheritance. It shall stick close to you like a garment through all eternity; it shall enter into your very bowels and search into the very marrow of your bones. A curse upon your eyes, never to see the least glimpse of comforting light; a curse upon your ears, to be entertained for all eternity with frightful shrieks and groans; a curse upon your taste, to be forever embittered with the gall of dragons; a curse upon your smell, to be always tormented with the noisome stench of the pit of Hell; a curse upon your feeling and on all the members of your body, to burn and yet never to be consumed in that fire which shall never be quenched; a curse upon your understanding, never to be enlightened with any ray of truth; a curse upon your memory, to be always revolving in the bitterness of a too late and a fruitless repentance for the shortness and vanity of past pleasures; a curse upon the imagination, ever representing present and future miseries; a curse upon the will, obstinate in evil, torn in pieces with a thousand violent and withal opposite desires, and unable to accomplish any one of them; a curse, at last, upon the whole soul, to be a hell to itself for all eternity!" Good God! Let it never be our misfortune to incur this dreadful curse!

Consider fifthly how, after the sentence is given, the elect shall enter without delay upon the possession of that everlasting Kingdom which God has prepared for those that serve Him, where sorrow can have no place and joy no end. But as for the wicked, the earth shall immediately open and swallow them all down at once, with the devils who seduced them, into the bottomless pit, and the gate shall be shut, never, never more to be opened! This is the end of all worldly pride. This is the end of all carnal pleasure. Oh, "*It is a fearful thing to fall into the hands of the living God!*" (*Hebrews* 10:31).

Chapter 13

On Hell

The Thirteenth Day

CONSIDER FIRST, as it is said in Holy Writ, *"That eye hath not seen, nor ear heard, neither hath it entered into the heart of man, what things God hath prepared for them that love him."* (*1 Corinthians* 2:9). So we may truly say with regard to the torments of Hell that no mortal tongue can express or heart conceive them. Beatitude, according to the theologians, is a "perfect and never-ending state, comprising at once all that is good, without any mixture of evil." If then damnation be the opposite to beatitude, it must needs be an everlasting deluge of all that is evil, without the least mixture of good, without the least alloy of ease, without the least glimpse of comfort—a total privation of all happiness and a chaos of all misery.

Consider secondly and more in particular what damnation is and how many and how great are the miseries which it involves: A dying life, or rather, a living death; a darksome prison, a loathsome dungeon, a binding of hand and foot in eternal chains; a land of horror and misery; a lake of fire and brimstone; a bottomless pit; devouring flames; a serpent ever gnawing; a worm that never dies; a body always burning and never consumed; a feeling always fresh for suffering; a thirst never extinguished; perpetual weeping, wailing and gnashing of

41

teeth; no other company but devils and damned wretches, all hating and cursing one another, all hating and cursing God; spirits always in an agony and sick to death, yet never meeting with this death which they so much desire; cast forth from the face of God into the land of oblivion; none to comfort, none to pity them; wounded to the heart with the sense of lost happiness and oppressed with the feeling of present misery; and all these sufferings everlasting, without the least hope of end, of intermission or of abatement. This is a short description, drawn for the most part from God's unerring word, of the miseries which eternal damnation imports. This is the bitter *"cup"* of which *"all the sinners of the earth shall drink."* (*Psalm* 74:9).

Consider thirdly that God in all His attributes is infinite: as in His power, wisdom, goodness, etc., so also in His avenging justice. He is a God in Hell as much as in Heaven, so that by the greatness of His love, mercy and patience here, we may measure the greatness of His future wrath and vengeance against impenitent sinners hereafter. By His infinite goodness He has drawn them out of nothing; He has preserved and sustained them for a long time; He has even come down from His throne of glory and allowed Himself to be nailed to a disgraceful cross for their eternal salvation. He has frequently delivered them from the dangers to which they were daily exposed, patiently borne with their insolence and repeated treasons, still graciously inviting them to repentance. Ah, how justly does His patience, so long abused, turn at length into fury! Mercy at last gives place to justice, and a thousand woes to those wretches who must forever feel the dreadful weight of the avenging hand of the living God!

Consider fourthy and—in order to understand somewhat better what Hell is—set before your eyes a poor sick man lying on his bed, burning with a pestilential fever, attended with a universal pain over all his body: his head perfectly rent asunder, his eyes ready to fly out, his teeth raging, his sides pierced with dreadful pains, his belly racked with violent cramps, his bowels with the stone and gravel, all his limbs tormented with rheumatic pains, and all his joints with gout, his heart even bursting with anguish, and him crying out for a drop of water to cool his tongue. Could anything be conceived more miserable? And yet this is but an imperfect picture of what the damned must endure for eternity, where these victims, immolated to the justice of God, *"shall be salted with fire"* (*Mark* 9:48) and shall endure in all the senses and members of their bodies and in all the faculties of their souls most exquisite torments!

Consider fifthly that the state of the poor sick man of whom we have just now been speaking—howsoever deplorable it may seem—might still be capable of some alleviation or ease, or some degree of comfort: a good bed to lie on, a good friend to encourage or condole with him, a good conscience to support him, a will resigned to the will of God, and in the end, a certain knowledge that his pains must shortly either abate or put an end to his life. But the damned enjoy nothing of all this. Their bed in Hell is a lake or pit burning with fire and brimstone, to which they are fastened down with eternal chains. Their companions are merciless devils or—what will be to them worse than devils—the unhappy partners of their sins! Their conscience is ever gnawed with the worm that never dies. Their will is averse from God and continually struggling in vain with His Divine Will. And what comes in to complete their damnation is a despair of ever meeting with an end or abatement of their torments. Good God! What would not a prudent man do to prevent lying, even for one night, in such torments in this life? And where then is our faith or reason when we will do so little to escape the dreadful night of Hell's merciless flames?

Chapter 14

On the Exterior Pains of Hell

The Fourteenth Day

CONSIDER FIRST the description which holy Job gives us of Hell when he calls it *"a land that is dark and covered with the mist of death: a land of misery and darkness, where the shadow of death and no order, but everlasting horror, dwelleth."* (*Job* 10:21-22). In this gloomy region, no sun, no moon, no stars appear; no comforting rays of light—not even the least glimpse—are ever to be seen. The very fire that burns there, contrary to the natural property of that element, is black and darksome and affords no light to the wretches it torments, except to reveal to them such objects as may increase their misery. Christians, what would you think were you to be sentenced to pass the remainder of your days in some horrid dungeon or hole, deep under ground, where you should never see the light? Would not death itself be preferable to such a punishment? And what is this to that eternal night to which the damned are sentenced? The Egyptians of Moses' time were in a sad condition when for three days the whole kingdom was covered with a dreadful darkness, caused by such gross exhalations that they might even be felt by the hand. But this misery was soon over, and they were comforted by the return of light. Not so the damned in Hell, whose night shall never have a morning or ever expect the dawning of day!

Consider secondly that the horror of this eternal night shall be aggravated beyond measure by the dismal music with which those poor wretches shall be forever entertained in this melancholy abode—which shall be none other than dreadful curses and blasphemies, the insulting voices of their tormentors and the howlings, groans and shrieks of the tormented, etc. And that the other senses may also come in for their share of misery, the smell shall be forever regaled with the loathsome exhalations of those infernal dungeons and the intolerable stench of those half-putrefied carcasses which are broiling there. The taste shall be oppressed with a most ravenous hunger and thirst, and the feeling with an unbearable fire.

Consider thirdly that of all the bodily torments which we can suffer in this world, there is none more terrible than to burn alive. But alas! There is no comparison between burning here and burning in Hell. All our fires upon earth are but painted flames, if compared to the fire of Hell. The fire of this world was made to serve us and to be our comfort; that of Hell was created to be an instrument of God's vengeance upon sinners. The fire of this world cannot subsist without being nourished by some combustible matter, which it quickly dispatches and consumes. The fire of Hell, kindled by the breath of an angry God, requires no other fuel than sin and feeds on this without ever decaying or consuming. Oh, Dreadful Stain of Sin, which suffices to maintain an everlasting fire! The fire of this world can only reach the body; the fire of Hell reaches the soul itself and fills it with most exquisite torments. Ah, Sinners, which of you all can dwell with this devouring fire? Which of you all can endure this eternal burning? (Cf. *Isaias* 33:14).

Consider fourthly, and—in order to frame some better notion of the torments of Hell—give ear to a most authentic vision related by St. Teresa of Avila in chapter 32 of her *Life*. "As I was one day in prayer," says the Saint, "all of a sudden I found myself in Hell. I know not how I was carried there, only I understood that Our Lord was pleased that I should see the place which the devils had prepared for me there and which I had deserved by my sins. What passed here with me lasted but a very little while, yet if I should live many years, I do not believe I should ever be able to forget it. The entrance appeared to me to resemble that of an oven, very low, very narrow and very dark. The ground seemed like mire, exceedingly filthy, stinking, insupportable and full of a multitude of loathsome vermin. At the end of it, there was a certain hollow place, as if it had been a kind of a little press in a wall, into which I found myself thrust and closely pent up. Now, though all this which I have said was far more terrible in itself than I have described it, yet it might pass for a pleasure in comparison with that which I felt in this press: this torment was so dreadful that no words can express the least part of it. I felt my soul burning in so dismal a fire that I am not able to describe it. I have experienced the most insupportable pains (in the judgment of physicians) which can be endured corporally in this world—as well by the shrinking up of all my sinews, as by many other torments of several kinds—but all these were nothing in comparison to what I suffered there, joined to the horrid thought that this was to be without end or intermission forever. And even this itself is still little if compared to the agony the soul is in."

It seems to her that she is choked, that she is stifled, and her anguish and torture go to a degree of excess that cannot be expressed. It is too little to say that it seems to her that she is butchered and rent to pieces, because this would express some violence from without which tended to her destruction; whereas, here it is that she herself is her own executioner and tears herself to pieces.

"Now as to the interior fire and unspeakable despair which come in to complete so many horrid torments, I admit I am not able to describe them. I saw not what it was that tormented me, but I perceived myself to burn, and at the same time to be cut, as it were, and hashed in pieces. In so frightful a place, there was no room for the least hope of comfort; there was no such thing as even sitting or lying down. I was thrust into a hole in a wall, and those horrible walls close in upon the poor prisoners and press and stifle them. There is nothing but thick darkness, without any mixture of light, and yet I know not how it is that, though there be no light, yet one sees there all that may be most mortifying to the sight. Although it be about six years since this happened which I here relate, I am even now, in writing it, so terrified that my blood chills in my veins; so that whatsoever evils or pains I now suffer, if I do but call to my remembrance what I then endured, all that can be suffered here appears to me simply nothing." So far the Saint's narration, which deserves to be pondered at leisure, for if such and so terrible torments had been prepared for her whose life from her cradle had been so innocent—setting aside a few worldly vanities, which for a short time she had followed—what must sinners one day expect?

Consider fifthly that there is no man on earth (who has not lost his senses) who would be willing, even for the empire of the world, to be broiled like St. Lawrence on a gridiron, or roasted for half an hour by a slow fire, though he were sure to come off with his life. Nay, where is the man who would even venture to hold his finger in the flame of a candle for half a quarter of an hour, for any reward that this world can give? Where is then the judgment of the far greater part of Christians, who pretend to believe in a Hell yet live on for years on end in the guilt of mortal sin with so little apprehension and concern, in danger every moment of falling into this dreadful and everlasting fire, having no more than a hair's breadth— that is, the thin thread of an uncertain life—between their lives and a miserable eternity? Good God, deliver us from this unfortunate blindness, from this desperate folly and madness!

Chapter 15

On the Interior Pains of Hell

The Fifteenth Day

CONSIDER FIRST that the fire of Hell, with all the rest of the exterior torments which are endured there, are terrible indeed, but are by no means comparable to the interior pains of the soul, that *pœna damni*— "pain of the damned," or eternal loss of God and of all that is good, that extremity of anguish which follows from this loss, that rueful remorse of a bitter but fruitless repentance accompanied by everlasting despair and rage, that combination of all those racking tortures in the inward powers and faculties of the soul—these are torments incomparably greater than anything that can be suffered in the body.

Consider secondly, in particular, that pain of loss, which, in the judgment of theologians, is the greatest of all the torments of Hell, though worldlings here have difficulties in conceiving how this can be. Alas, poor sinners, so weak is their notion of eternal goods and so deeply are they immersed in the things of this world—amusing themselves with the vanity of created objects, which divert their thoughts from God's sovereign goodness— that they cannot imagine that this loss of God can be so great and dismal a torment, as the Saints and servants of God, who are guided by better lights, all agree it is! But the case will be quite altered when they shall find themselves in Hell. There they shall be convinced by their own woeful experience what a misery it is to have lost their God, to have lost Him totally, to have lost Him irrecoverably, to have lost Him eternally, to have lost Him in Himself, to have lost Him in all His creatures, to be eternally banished from Him who was their Only Happiness, their Last End and Sovereign Good, the Overflowing Fountain of all good; and in losing Him, to have lost all that *is* good—and that forever. As long as sinners are in this mortal life, they in many ways partake of the goodness of God, who makes the sun to rise upon the good and bad and rains upon the just and unjust. All that is agreeable in this world, all that is delightful in creatures, and all that is comfortable in life, is all, in some measure, a participation in the Divine Goodness. Is it no wonder, then, that the sinner, while he in so many ways partakes of the goodness of God, should not in this life be aware of what it is to be totally and eternally deprived of Him. But in Hell, alas, those unhappy wretches shall find that, in losing their God, they have also lost every kind of good or comfort which any of His creatures heretofore afforded—instead of which, they find all things now conspiring against them and there being no way left of diverting the dreadful thought of this loss, which is always present to their minds and grips them with inexpressible torments.

Consider thirdly that every damned soul shall be a Hell unto herself, and all and every one of her powers and faculties shall have their respective hells. Her *memory* shall be forever tormented by revolving without ceasing the thought of her past folly, stupidity and madness in forfeiting the eternal joys of Heaven—that ocean of bliss which she might have obtained at so cheap a price and of which so many of her acquaintance are now in possession—exchanged for an empty, trifling pleasure that lasted but for a moment and left nothing behind it except the stain of sin and the remorse of a guilty conscience, or for some petty interest or punctilio of honor by which she was then robbed of all her treasures and all true honor, and upon account of which she is now so miserable, poor and despicable, eternally trodden underfoot by insulting devils. Oh, what will her judgment then be of this transitory world and all its cheating vanities, when after having been millions of ages in Hell, looking back from that immense eternity and being scarcely able to discern in that infinite duration this little point of her mortal life, she shall compare time and eternity, past pleasures and present pains, virtue and vice, Heaven and Hell!

Consider fourthly that the *understanding* of the damned shall also have its hell, in being forever deprived of the light of truth, always employed in false and blasphemous judgments and notions concerning God and His justice, to the great increase of its own misery, and will be ever dwelling upon the thoughts of present and future torments, without being able for a moment to think of anything else; so that all and every one of the torments which the damned endure, and are to endure for eternity, are every moment before the eyes of their understanding; and thus, in every moment, they bear the insupportable load of a miserable eternity.

Consider fifthly that, as the obstinate *will* of the sinner has been the most guilty, so this power of the soul shall suffer in proportion the greatest torments, always seeking what she shall never find and ever flying from what she must forever endure! Ah, what fruitless longings, what vain wishes shall be her constant entertainment, while she is doomed for eternity, never to attain to any one of them or to the least thing which she desires! Oh, who can express that violent impetuosity with which the will of these wretches is now carried towards God, aware as they are now of the immense happiness which is found in the enjoyment of Him? But, alas! They always find an invisible hand that drives them back; or rather, they always find themselves bound down fast in eternal chains, struggling in vain with that hand which they cannot resist and unable to make the least approach toward the object of their restless desires. Hence, they break forth into a thousand blasphemies; hence, the whole soul is torn to pieces with a whole army of violent and withal opposite passions—of fury, envy, hatred, despair, etc. These torments of the interior powers of the soul are accompanied by the never-dying worm of conscience, which shall forever prey upon those miscreants, by which is meant an eternal remorse, a bitter but fruitless repentance, which is ever racking their despairing souls. *Sweet Jesus, deliver us from such a dreadful combination of evils!*

Chapter 16

On a Miserable Eternity

The Sixteenth Day

CONSIDER FIRST that what above all things makes Hell intolerable is the eternity of its torments. It is this eternity that is an infinite aggravation to all and every one of them who suffer there. It is this bitter ingredient that makes so unbearable every drop of that bitter cup of the divine vengeance of which the sinners of the earth must drink. Were there any hope that the miseries of the damned would one day have an end, though it were after millions of ages, Hell would be no longer Hell, because it would admit of some comfort. But for all those inexpressible torments to continue forever, as long as God shall be God, without the least hope of ever seeing an end of them—oh, this it is that is the greatest torment of the damned! O Eternity, Eternity, how little do worldlings comprehend thee now! But how terrible wilt thou be to them one day when they shall find themselves engulfed in the bottomless abyss, there to be forever the butt and mark of all the arrows of God's avenging justice!

Consider secondly, that if one short night seems so long and tedious to a poor sick man in a burning fever, if he tosses and turns and nowhere finds rest, if he counts every hour and with so much impatience longs for the morning, which yet will bring him but little relief or comfort, what must this dreadful night of eternity be, accompanied by all the interior and exterior torments of Hell! No man in his senses would purchase even a kingdom at the rate of lying for ten years on a soft bed without coming off it. Ah! What misery then must it be to be chained down to a bed of fire and brimstone, not for ten years only, nor yet for ten thousand times ten years, but for as many hundred thousand millions of ages, as there are drops of water in the ocean or atoms in the air—in a word, for an immense eternity.

Consider thirdly, and in order to conceive still better what this eternity is, imagine to yourself that, if any one of the damned were to shed but one single tear at the end of every thousand years, till he had shed tears enough to fill the sea, what an immense space of time must this require? The world has not yet lasted six thousand years, so that the first of all the damned would not have shed six tears. And yet, Oh Dreadful Eternity! The time will certainly come, when any one of those wretches that are now in Hell will be able with truth to say that, at the rate of one tear for a thousand years, he might have shed tears enough to drown the whole world and fill up the immense space between Heaven and earth; and happy would he be if his torments were *then* to have an end. But alas, after these millions of millions of ages, he shall be as far from the end of his misery as he was the first day he fell into Hell! Compute after this, if you please, as many hundred thousand millions of years as your thoughts can reach to; nay, suppose the whole surface of the earth to be covered with numeral figures; and figure up, if you can, this immense sum of years, and then multiply it by itself and multiply again a second time the product by itself; and then at the foot of this immense number write down, *"Here begins eternity!"* O Terrible Eternity! Is it possible that they who believe in thee should not fear thee? Is it possible, that they who fear thee should dare to sin?*

---

*All these comparisons of the enormous lengths of time given here as contrasted to eternity are helpful to enable us to realize that there is

Consider fourthly that, in this eternity, it would be some small comfort to the damned if their pains, like those of this life, had any intermission or abatement. But alas, their torments are always the same; their eternal fever never abates! For as their sins are always the same and the gate of mercy and pardon is eternally shut upon them, so the punishment of their sins shall always continue in one and the same degree of rigor, without the least remission or diminution. The rich glutton in Hell (Cf. *Luke* 16:19-31) has not yet been able to obtain so much as that single drop of water for which he so earnestly begged, nor will he ever obtain it for all eternity. Nor shall length of time inure those wretches to those evils which they suffer, in order to make them the more bearable, nor will routine and custom harden them against them; but after millions of ages, their torments shall be as fresh and their feeling of them the same as on the first day. O Great God! Who can bear Thine indignation or support the weight of Thine avenging hand? Oh dreadful evil of mortal sin, which alone can enkindle this eternal flame!

---

actually *no* real comparison between time (however long) and eternity. Catholic philosophers and theologians have often explained that Heaven and Hell are really *"a perpetual now,"* and truly do not admit of time, which in the Scholastic philosophers' definition is a "measure of motion, according to before and after," and is actually an intellectual construct created by man's intelligence to demarcate events in life, where all that man experiences is motion and change. But God is unchanging and not subject to motion, and therefore not subject to or a part of time. Philosophers and theologians have mentally struggled with this mysterious disparity between time (man's experience) and eternity (the reality of God's life, which does not change). —*Publisher*, 2006.

Chapter 17

On Heaven

The Seventeenth Day

CONSIDER FIRST that, if God's justice be so terrible in regard to His enemies, how much more will His mercy, His goodness, His bounty declare themselves in favor of His friends! Mercy and goodness are His favorite attributes, in which He most delights: *"His tender mercies,"* says the Royal Prophet, *"are over all his works."* (*Psalm* 144:9). What then must be this blessed kingdom which, in His goodness, He has prepared for His beloved children, for the manifestation of His riches, His glory and His magnificence for all eternity—a kingdom which the Son of God Himself has purchased for us at no less a price than that of His own most Precious Blood? No wonder, then, that the Apostle cries out: *"That eye hath not seen, nor ear heard, neither hath it entered into the heart of man what things God hath prepared for them that love him."* (*1 Corinthians* 2:9). No wonder that this beatitude is defined by theologians as a perfect and everlasting state, filled with all that is good, without the least mixture of evil, a general and universal good, filling brim-full the vast capacity of our affections and desires, and eternally securing us from all fear or danger of need or change. Oh, here it is that the servants of God, as the Psalmist declares, *"shall be inebriated with the plenty of thy house, and thou shalt make them drink of the torrent*

55

of thy pleasure," (*Psalm* 35:9)—even of that *"fountain of life,"* (*Psalm* 35:10), which is with Him and flows from Him into their happy souls forever and ever!

Consider secondly that, although this blessed kingdom abounds with all that can be imagined to be good and delightful, yet there is one Sovereign Good, in the sight, love and enjoyment of which consists the essential beatitude of the soul, and that is God Himself, whom the Blessed ever see face to face, and by the contemplation of His infinite beauty are set on fire with seraphic flames of love, and by a most pure and amiable union are transformed in a manner into God Himself—as when brass or iron in the furnace is perfectly penetrated by the fire, it loses its own nature and becomes all flame and fire. Happy Souls! What can be wanting to complete your joys, you who are in perfect possession of your God, the overflowing Source of all Good, who have within and without you the vast ocean of endless felicity? Oh, the excessive bounty of our God, who giveth to His servants in reward for their loyalty so great a good, which is nothing less than Himself, the immense Joy of the Angels! Oh, shall that not suffice, my Soul, to make thee happy, which makes God Himself happy?

Consider thirdly the glory and beauty of Heaven, of this "heavenly Jerusalem," which Holy Scripture—to accommodate itself to our weakness—represents to us under the notion of such things as we most admire here below. Thus, St. John in the *Apocalypse,* describing this beautiful city, tells us that its walls are of precious stones and its streets of pure and transparent gold; that these streets are watered with the water of the river of life, resplendent as crystal, which flows from the throne of God; and that on the banks of this river, on both sides, grows the Tree of Life, that there shall be no night, nor any sun or moon, but that the Lord God shall be its light forever. O Blessed Jerusalem! Oh, how glorious are the things that are said of thee, O City of God! But what wonder is it really? For if our great God has given us such and so noble a palace here below, in this place of banishment, beautified with the sun, moon and stars, accomplished and furnished with this infinite variety of plants, flowers, trees and living creatures of so many sorts, all subservient to man—if, I say, He has so richly provided for us in this vale of tears and in this region of the shade of death, what must our eternal habitation be in the Land of the Living? If here He is so bountiful, even to His enemies, in giving them so commodious, so noble a dwelling, what may not His friends and servants expect in His eternal kingdom, in which and by which He designs to manifest to them His greatness and glory for endless ages, in an everlasting banquet which He has there prepared for His elect. Blessed by all creatures be His goodness forever!

Consider fourthly the blessed inhabitants of this heavenly kingdom, those millions of millions of Angels, of whom the prophet Daniel, having seen God Almighty in a vision, tells us that *"thousands of thousands ministered to him, and ten thousand times a hundred thousand stood before him,"* (*Daniel* 7:10)—that infinite multitude of Saints and martyrs and other servants of God of both sexes, gathered out of all nations, tribes and tongues; and above them all the Blessed Virgin, Mother of God, Queen of Saints and Angels. Their number is innumerable. But oh, who can express the happiness of enjoying this blessed company? They are all most noble, most glorious, most wise, most holy. They are all of blood royal, all kings and queens, all children and heirs of the Most High God, ever beautiful and ever young, crowned with wreaths of immortal glory and shining much more brightly than the sun. Their love and charity for one another are more than can be conceived: They all have but one heart, one will and one soul, so that the joy and satisfaction of every one are multiplied to as many-fold as there are blessed souls and Angels in Heaven, by the inexpressible delight that each one takes in the happiness of all and every one of the rest. Christians, let us imitate their virtues here, that we may come to their happy society hereafter, and with them eternally sing to our God the immortal songs of Sion!

Consider fifthly that what renders all the joys of Heaven and the felicity of the Blessed complete is the eternity of this bliss and that infallible certainty and security which they enjoy, that their happiness is even linked with God's eternity, that as long as God shall be God, they shall be with Him in His blessed kingdom. O my Soul, how pleasant, how delightful it is to look forward into this vast eternity and there to lose thyself in this happy prospect of endless ages!

Oh, bless thy God, who has prepared these immortal joys for the reward of such small services and designed them from all eternity for thee. Nor shall this immense eternity render these enjoyments in any way disagreeable or tedious by the length of the possession thereof, but as God is an endless ocean of all good and His divine essence an inexhaustible treasure of delights, so the happiness of those that eternally enjoy Him shall always be fresh, always new!

Conclude then, O Christian Soul, to hold in contempt and to forsake all that is earthly and temporal and from this hour to begin thy journey toward this glorious, heavenly and eternal kingdom. There thou shall find all that thy heart can desire: immortal honors, immense riches, pure and eternal pleasures, life, health, beauty never fading, etc. Oh, this alone is thy true home, the Land of the Living!

Chapter 18

On the Small Number
Of the Elect

The Eighteenth Day

CONSIDER FIRST those words of Christ, *"Many are called, but few [are] chosen,"* (*Matthew* 20:16), which contain a great and dreadful truth, frequently inculcated by the mouth of Truth Itself, to rouse unthinking mortals from their profound lethargy into which the enemy has lulled them. This is one of those lessons which He has laid down for a foundation of Christian morality in His divine Sermon on the Mount, where He tells us: *"Enter ye in at the narrow gate, for wide is the gate and broad is the way that leadeth to destruction, and many there are who go in thereat. How narrow is the gate and strait is the way that leadeth to life, and few there are that find it!"* (*Matthew* 7:13-14). Hence, in the same sermon, He declares to us, *"Not every one that saith to me, Lord, Lord, shall enter into the kingdom of heaven, but he that doth the will of my Father who is in heaven,"* (*Matthew* 7:21), that is, by a faithful compliance with the law of God and His Gospel. Without this, He assures us that it will avail us nothing even to have done miracles in His name: *"Many will say to me in that day [of judgment], Lord, Lord, have not we prophesied in thy name, and cast out devils in thy name, and done many miracles in thy name?*

*And then I will profess unto them, I never knew you;
depart from me, you that work iniquity."* (*Matthew* 7:22-
23). Good God! What will become of us, if those that have
even done miracles in Thy name shall nevertheless be
excluded from Thine eternal kingdom?*

Consider secondly in how many ways this frightful
truth has been declared or prefigured to us in the Old
Testament. Of all the inhabitants of the earth, only eight
souls—namely, Noah and his family—were preserved in
the Ark from the waters of the deluge; of six hundred
thousand [counting only the grown men] of the children
of Israel who came out of the land of Egypt under the
conduct of Moses, only two persons, Joshua and Caleb,
entered Canaan, the Land of Promise, which figure the
Apostle St. Paul expressly applies to us Christians. (Cf.
1 Corinthians 10:6). To the same effect, the prophet Isaias likens those that shall escape the divine vengeance to
that small number of olives that remains on the tree
after the fruit is gathered, or to the few bunches of grapes
that are found on the vines after a well-gleaned vintage.

---

*Here Our Saviour is referring principally to those heretics who seem
to follow Him under the name of Christian, but who deny the unity
of Faith and certain of His doctrines, even though in His name they
may have done "wonders" of healing and driving out devils. This dis-
avowal of certain "Christians" can also be predicated of any of us who
serve Our Lord with our lips, but our hearts are far from Him. (*"This
people honors me with their lips, but their heart is far from me."*—
Matthew 15:8). These qualifications of His meaning, nonetheless, do
not mitigate or dilute Our Lord's strong language about the relatively small number of those who are saved, nor concerning what
strict adherence to His commandments is required for salvation. In
the annals of the Saints, one often encounters their powerful state-
ments about the relatively small number of the saved. If the reader
is still not convinced by all of this, he should return to page 59 and
reread the quote from *Matthew* 7:13-14, especially the second sentence: *"How narrow is the gate and strait is the way that leadeth to
life, and* few *there are that find it."* Out of the mouth of our Divine
Saviour Himself—who by His divine, infinitely good nature can
speak *only* the truth—we have the confirmation that "few" even *find*
the "gate" "that leadeth to life," that is, to eternal salvation, let alone,
enter in and attain it. —*Publisher*, 2006.

(*Isaias* 24:13-14). Ah, Christians, hear then and obey the voice of your Saviour when He tells you, *"Strive to enter by the narrow gate, for many, I say to you, shall seek to enter and shall not be able,"* (*Luke* 13:24), because the generality of Christians, though they make some endeavors to enter, yet do not strive with all their strength; they are not thoroughly in earnest in their seeking and therefore shall never find the gate to eternal life. (*"Few there are that find it."—Matthew* 7:14). Hear again, with fear and trembling, the great Apostle St. Peter when he says, *"If the just man shall scarcely be saved, where shall the ungodly and the sinner appear?"* (*1 Peter* 4:18). O my Soul, let us then take care, as the same Apostle admonishes, *"that by good works you may make sure your calling and election."* (*2 Peter* 1:10). And if others will go in crowds to Hell, let us resolve not to go with them just to keep them company.

Consider thirdly that, even if the Scripture had said nothing of the small number of the elect, yet this truth must appear evident to us if we compare the lives of the generality of Christians with the Gospel of Christ and His holy commandments. *"But if thou wilt enter into life,"* says Our Lord, *"keep the commandments."* (*Matthew* 19:17). There is no other way to life everlasting. And the first and greatest of all the commandments is this: *"Thou shalt love the Lord thy God with all thy whole heart, and with thy whole soul, and with thy whole mind."* (*Matthew* 22:37). Now, how few are there that keep this commandment! It is easy to say with the generality of Christians that we love God with our whole heart, but what is the practice of our lives? Do not self-love, vainglory, sensuality, etc., on every occasion take the place of God in our lives? If so, it is vain to say that we love Him above all things. And yet, there is no salvation without this kind of love. **Think well on it!** Besides, the Apostle St. James declares that *"Whosoever therefore will be a friend of this world, becometh an enemy of God."* (*James* 4:4). And St. John says, *"If any man love the world, the charity of the*

Father is not in him." (*1 John* 2:15). And Christ Himself
declares that *"No man can serve two masters."* (*Matthew*
6:24). How then can we think to reconcile the conduct of
the greatest number of those who call themselves Christians—whose whole preoccupation is to please the world
and to conform themselves to its false maxims, corrupt
customs and deluding vanities—with their expectation of
attaining the Kingdom of Heaven, which is not to be
obtained except by using violence upon ourselves, by
renouncing this sinful world and by a life of self-denial
and mortification? (*"The kindom of heaven suffereth violence, and the violent bear it away."* —*Matthew* 11:12).

Consider fourthly how great a corruption is generally
found even among the greatest part of true believing
Christians, and from thence make a judgment of their
future lot.* How few are proof against human respect
and the pernicious fear of what the world will say! Alas!
What numbers sacrifice their eternal salvation to this
accursed fear by choosing to forfeit the grace of God
rather than the false honor and esteem of this world!
How many of those whose birth and fortune have
advanced them above the level of their fellow mortals
live continually in the state of damnation (the state of
mortal sin) by a cursed disposition of never putting up
with an affront and of preferring their worldly honor
before their conscience! Unhappy men who—by conform-
ing themselves now to these false maxims of deluded
worldlings—will be trampled underfoot by insulting devils for all eternity! How few masters of families are sincerely solicitous for those under their charge, to see that
instruction is not wanting, devotions not neglected, etc.,
and that nothing scandalous or sinful lurks under the

---

*Bishop Challoner of course is not advising the reader to judge where
the souls of individuals will go for all eternity, but rather is com-
menting that the observable conduct of many Catholics involves acts
and omissions which are objectively mortally sinful—and by Faith
we know that unrepented mortal sin is punished by eternal damnation. —*Publisher*, 2006.

favor of their negligence or co-operation. And yet the Apostle assures us that, if any man neglect the care of his family, he is worse than an infidel. (Cf. *1 Timothy* 5:8). How few parents effectually take care to bring up their children from their infancy in the fear of God and at an early age to inspire in them the horror of sin above all evils! Ah, what a double damnation will the greatest part bring upon themselves by sacrificing to the world and the devil these tender souls whom they might with so much ease have consecrated to Heaven! In short, not to cover all states of life in particular, is it not visible that injustice, impurity, pride, detraction, etc., everywhere reign among Christians and that the number of those who live up to the Gospel is very small? Good God, have mercy on us, and give us grace to be of the number of the few, that so we may be of the number of the saved!*

---

*A simple mathematical way of stating this situation comes from Fr. Sarda y Salvany's book *Liberalism is a Sin*. Catholics compose about 17% of the world's population, based on today's figures. Given that perhaps only 5% of Catholics are ardent in their faith, that computes to about one-half of one percent of the world's population who are seriously working toward their salvation. Even multiplying this by five times, to take into account a margin of error, and still one would arrive at only two and one-half percent of the world's population is seriously striving for salvation. Few indeed even then! And a sobering thought. —*Publisher*, 2006.

Chapter 19

On Mortal Sin

The Nineteenth Day

CONSIDER FIRST that there is not upon earth, nor even in Hell itself, a monster more hideous, more filthy and abominable, than mortal sin—a monster that is the first-born of the devil, or to speak more properly, is the parent both of the devil and Hell. There was not in the whole universe a creature more beautiful, more perfect, more accomplished with all kinds of gifts—both of nature and of grace—than was that bright Angel Lucifer and his companions! Yet one mortal sin, and that a sin consented to only in thought, changed them in an instant into ugly devils, just objects of horror and abomination to God and man. What effect, think ye, will sin have upon man, who is but dust and ashes, if it blasted so foully the "stars of heaven?" It was this monster, sin, that cast our first parents out of Paradise and condemned both them and their posterity to innumerable miseries, and to both a temporal and an eternal death. It was sin that drowned the world with the waters of the Flood and which daily crowds Hell with millions of poor souls, to be the fuel of endless flames. Good God, deliver us from this accursed evil!

Consider secondly that mortal sin is the death of the soul. For as it is the soul of a man which gives life to his body—and consequently that body is dead from which the soul is gone—so it is the grace of God which is the life of the soul, and that soul is dead which by mortal sin has lost her God and His Sanctifying Grace. If then a dead carcass from which the soul is gone, be so loathsome and frightful that few could endure to pass one night in the same bed with such a bed-fellow, how is it possible, Unhappy Sinner, that thou canst endure to carry continually about with thee the carcass of a soul dead in mortal sin, which is far more loathsome and hideous? Ah, beg of God that He would open thine eyes to see thine own deplorable state, to detest the hellish monster, sin, which thou hast so long nourished in thy breast and which is the true cause of all thy misery!

Consider thirdly what the soul loses by mortal sin and what she gains to recompense this loss. She loses the grace of God—Sanctifying Grace—the greatest of all treasures, and in losing this, she loses God Himself; she loses the fatherly protection and favor of God; she loses the dignity of being a child of God and spouse of Christ; she loses her right and title to an eternal kingdom; she is stripped of all the gifts of the Holy Ghost; robbed of all the merits of her whole life; becomes a child of Hell and a slave of the devil, spiritually possessed by him and with him liable to an eternal damnation. And this is all she gains by sin, because *"the wages of sin is death,"* (*Romans* 6:23), the death of the soul here, and a second and eternal death hereafter. Ah, Wretched Sinners, open your eyes to see and bewail your lamentable blindness in thus exchanging God for the devil, in exchanging Heaven for Hell.

Consider fourthly that sin is infinitely odious and detestable in the sight of God, as being infinitely opposite to His Sovereign Goodness. He hates it with an eternal and necessary hatred and can no more cease to hate it than He can cease to be God. Hence, if the most just man upon earth were so unhappy as to fall into any one of the least mortal sins, he would in that same moment become the enemy of God. And if he were to die in that guilt, he would certainly feel the weight of God's avenging justice for all eternity. Ah, Christians, never let us be so mad as to venture to be at war with God. Alas! How many and how dreadful judgments does He daily exercise upon sin and sinners! How many, in punishment of sin, are snatched away in the flower of their age by a sudden and unprovided death! How many die in despair! How many, after having long abused God's graces, are given up to a reprobate sense, to a hardness of heart, the worst and most terrible of all His judgments! Oh, let us tremble at the thought of so great a misfortune; let us be convinced that there can be no misery so great as that which we incur by mortal sin and that we are more our own enemies and do ourselves more harm by consenting to any one mortal sin, than all the men upon earth and all the devils in Hell could do us, though they were all to conspire together to do their worst, because all that they can do, as long as we do not consent to sin, cannot hurt the soul; whereas, we ourselves, by consenting to any one mortal sin, bring upon our own souls a dreadful and eternal death. Good God, never suffer us to be so blind as to become thus the murderers of our own souls!

Consider fifthly, O my Soul, and tremble at the sight of that multitude of treasons against thy God by which thou hast so often provoked His indignation in the whole course of thy life. Alas! Is it not too true that thou no sooner camest to the use of reason than thou didst abandon thy King and thy God, under the wings of whose fatherly protection thou hadst happily passed the days of thine innocence? Ah, how early didst thou run away from the best of fathers, and like the Prodigal Son, squandering away thy substance in a strange land, seek in vain to satisfy thine appetite with the husks of swine! Pass over in thy memory, in the bitterness of thy soul, all the years of thy life, and see what treasures of iniquity in thought, word and deed will reveal themselves to thine eyes; see how long thou hast unconcernedly sported thyself on the brink of a dreadful precipice, having no more than a hair's breadth between thy soul and Hell. Be confounded at thy past folly; admire and adore the goodness of thy God; and now, at least, resolve to embrace His mercy!

Chapter 20

On the Relapsing Sinner

The Twentieth Day

CONSIDER FIRST that if any single mortal sin be so heinous a treason against the Sovereign Majesty of God, as we have seen in the foregoing chapter, if every such sin be an abomination to Our Lord and the death of the soul of that unhappy sinner who is guilty of it, what must we think of the miserable condition of relapsing sinners, that is, of such Christians who are continually falling, again and again, into the same mortal sins, after repeated Confessions and solemn promises of amendment? Alas! What can we think, except that by this method of life they are treasuring up to themselves wrath against the Day of Wrath and will in all appearance sooner or later draw down a dreadful vengeance upon their own heads—because by every relapse their crime is aggravated and their latter condition becomes worse than the former.

Consider secondly the ingratitude, the perfidiousness, the contempt of God, of which the relapsing sinner is guilty, as often as—after his reconciliation—he returns to his sin, like the dog to his vomit. *"As a dog that returneth to his vomit, so is the fool that repeateth his folly."* —*Proverbs* 26:11. He is guilty of the highest ingratitude in treading underfoot the grace of reconciliation by which, a little before, he had been raised from the dunghill of sin and even drawn out of the jaws of Hell, and by a distinguishing mercy restored to the friendship of God and to the dignity of a child of God and an heir of Heaven. He is guilty of a base perfidiousness in breaking his solemn word given to God in his Confession. He is guilty of a notorious contempt of the Divine Majesty in banishing God from his soul, after having invited Him in, and introducing Satan in his place—and this after a full knowledge and experience of both sides. O Good God, to put the whole universe in balance with Thee would be a most heinous affront, since Heaven and all the powers thereof, the earth and seas and all things therein are less than a grain of sand if compared to Thee! What then must we think of the unparalleled injury done Thee by the relapsing sinner when, putting Thee and Satan in the scales, he gives the preference to the devil?

Consider thirdly the dreadful danger to which the relapsing sinner is daily exposed from the sword of the Divine Justice hanging over his guilty head and daily provoked by his ingratitude and insolence. Alas, we are all mortal! we know neither the day nor the hour that will be our last; and if we be surprised by death in the state of mortal sin, as millions have been, we are irrecoverably lost. If then it be a madness at any time to risk eternity by consenting to mortal sin, how much more to provoke the Almighty by frequent relapses and by a practice of abusing His grace and mercy at every turn! Ah, what multitudes of souls have been thus betrayed into that dismal pit of never-ending woe, *"where their worm dieth not, and the fire is not extinguished."* (*Mark* 9:43). Unhappy wretches! They planned as little to damn themselves as any of us, but God will not be laughed at. *"Be not deceived; God is not mocked!"*—(*Galatians* 6:7).

Consider fourthly another evil which the sinner who frequently falls back into the same sins has with just reason to be aware of, which is the insincerity of his past repentance. For in reality, what appearance is there that his sorrow and resolution of amendment have been such as God requires when, after so many Confessions, he is still the same man? True contrition is a *sovereign grief,* by which the penitent detests his sins above all other evils, with a full determination and firm resolution of never returning to them anymore. Now, how is it likely that the relapsing sinner detests sincerely his sin above all evils, with a firm purpose of amendment, when he is so soon and so easily prevailed upon by the first temptation to return to it again?

Consider fifthly the remedies and means by which we are to be preserved from this pernicious evil of relapsing into mortal sin. The first is to avoid the dangerous occasions which have drawn us, or probably may draw us, into the same sins. Without this care to flee from the occasions of sin, the strongest resolutions of amendment will prove ineffectual, as we daily see by woeful experience; for *"He that loveth danger shall perish in it." (Ecclesiasticus* 3:27). No pretexts of worldly concerns must here be put into the balance with eternity; we must part with hand or eye sooner than lose our souls! *"And if thy right eye scandalize thee, pluck it out and cast it from thee. For it is expedient for thee that one of thy members should perish, rather than that thy whole body be cast into hell. And if thy right hand scandalize thee, cut it off and cast it from thee, for it is expedient for thee that one of thy members should perish, rather than that thy whole body go into hell."* (Cf. *Matthew* 5:29-30).

Another main preservative against relapse is to labor by fervent prayer and diligent frequenting of the Sacraments to suppress the unhappy dispositions that insensibly lead to sin, vigorously to resist the first motions to evil, and to strive with all possible diligence to root out that wretched propensity to sin which former sins have left in the soul. Ah, how hard it is to maintain a castle where the enemy has already captured the avenues of approach and has a strong party within, ready to open the gates unto them!

The third and chief remedy against relapse is that the

penitent carefully nourish in his heart a truly penitential spirit, daily renew his sorrow for his sins, and recount in the sight of God in the bitterness of his soul all his past iniquities; daily admire and adore that mercy which has borne with him so long, and value above all treasures that grace of reconciliation by which he has been drawn out of so much misery; and daily beg of God, with all the fervor of his soul, sooner to take him out of this world than to allow him anymore to die to Him by mortal sin. Good God, grant that this may always be the disposition of our souls! *Amen, amen!*

Chapter 21

On Doing Penance for Our Sins

The Twenty-First Day

CONSIDER FIRST those words of Christ, *"Unless you shall do penance, you shall all likewise perish."* (*Luke* 13:3, 5). Behold here a general rule, nor does our Lord make any exception. Penance then is necessary, *first*, for all those whose conscience accuses them of mortal sin. Alas! Such as these must either do penance for their sins or burn for them for all eternity. Poor sinners! Their state is most deplorable; they are playing upon the brink of Hell, and every moment one or other of them is tumbling down into that bottomless pit. And is it possible that they should be unconcerned under so great and evident a danger? Why then do they not lay hold of the grace of penance, the only plank that can save them after shipwreck, the only means left for the salvation of their souls.

Secondly, penance is necessary for all those who, though their conscience accuses them not at present, yet have in their past life been guilty of such mortal offenses. Ah, Christians, any single mortal sin is enough for us to do penance for all our life! And how can we do less, if we consider what mortal sin is, what it is to have been the enemies of God, what it is to have been under the sentence of eternal damnation and never with certitude to know whether this sentence has been cancelled?* Is not this sufficient to oblige us to a penitential life? Can we otherwise pretend to be secure? Even those (and God best knows how few they are) who are not conscious to themselves of having committed any such sin in their whole lifetime must not therefore think themselves exempt from the obligation of doing penance, as well because of their hidden sins as those which they may have occasioned in others, for *"man knoweth not whether he be worthy of love or hatred,"* (*Ecclesiastes* 9:1), but also because a penitential life is the best security against sin, which will insensibly prevail over us if not curbed by self-denial, mortification and penance.

Consider secondly that, as to the method of penance, different rules must be prescribed to different persons. Those who have the misfortune to be actually in the state of mortal sin or—what is still more deplorable—who are plunged in the depth of a habit of one or more kinds of mortal sin, as soon as their eyes are opened to discover the hellish monster which they carry about with them, must, like the Prodigal Son, arise without delay to return to their Father. The sacrifice of a contrite and humble heart is what God, above all things, calls for at their hands; this ought to be the foundation of all their penance. Without this, corporal austerities will be of small account. Such sinners ought to give themselves no rest until they have made their peace with their God. Their sin ought to be always before their eyes. Their first thoughts in the morning ought to be upon their misfortune in being at so great a distance from their God,

---

*The Council of Trent states that, without a special revelation from God, one cannot know with absolute certitude that he is in the state of grace. The main cause of this uncertainty would be a person's lack of absolute certitude regarding the adequacy of his contrition or his firm purpose of amendment in the Sacrament of Penance. Yet a Catholic is not supposed to be anxious over this absence of positive assurance that he is in the state of grace, but rather, he should be honest with God and with himself and trust in God for the help he needs to know his sins and overcome them. —*Publisher*, 2006.

enslaved to the devil, and liable to be his companions in eternal misery. The like ought to be their last thoughts at night when, as the penitent David, they ought to "wash their beds with their tears." As often as they appear before their God in prayer, it ought to be in the spirit of the humble publican, looking upon themselves as unworthy to raise their eyes to Heaven or toward the altar of God, and with him, striking their breasts with an *"O God, be merciful to me, a sinner."* (*Luke* 18:13). Thus will they certainly obtain mercy from Him who is the Father of mercy.

Consider thirdly that, after the sinner has made his endeavors to seek a reconciliation with his offended God by a sincere repentance and confession of his sins, he must not think himself exempt from any further penance, as if he had now no just debt to discharge to the justice of God, no obligation of making satisfaction for his sins by penitential works, and of bringing forth fruits worthy of penance. *"Bring forth therefore fruits worthy of penance."* (*Luke* 3:8). This would be a great and dangerous error. Nor must he content himself with barely carrying out the penance enjoined by his confessor, which it is to be feared is seldom sufficient to satisfy fully the justice of God. Alas! If sinners were truly aware of the enormous injury [i.e., insult] done to God by mortal sin, as true penitents must be, they would certainly do penance in another manner than too many do; they would be more in earnest in chastising their own sinful flesh by penitential works and thus making a more proportionate satisfaction for their past treasons.

Consider fourthly that the true manner of doing penance for our sins is better learned from the holy Fathers and Doctors of the Church than from the loose maxims of worldlings or the practice of too many penitents in this degenerate age. Let us give ear, then, to those lights of the Church and follow their directions on this important subject. "God himself has taught us," says St. Cyprian, "in what manner we are to beg mercy of

Him. He Himself says, *'Be converted to me with all your heart, in fasting and in weeping and in mourning.'* (*Joel* 2:12). Let us then return to the Lord with our whole heart; let us appease His wrath by fasting, weeping and mourning, as He admonishes us. Let the greatness of our grief equal the heinousness of our sins. We must pray earnestly; we must pass the day in mourning and the night in watching and weeping, spending all our time in penitential tears. Our lodging should be on the floor, strewed with ashes, our covering hair-cloth, etc. After having cast off the garment of Christ, we should not now seek any worldly clothing. We must employ ourselves now in good works, by which our sins may be purged away. We must give frequent alms, by which our souls may be delivered from death." (*L. de Lapis*). So far St. Cyprian, with whom St. Pacian agrees in his *Exhortation to Penance:* "If any one call you to the bath, you must renounce all such delights. If any one invite you to a banquet, you must say, 'such invitations are for those that have not had the misfortune to lose their God. I have sinned against the Lord and am in danger of perishing eternally. What have I to do with feasts, who have offended my God?' You must make your court to the poor; you must beg the prayers of widows; you must cast yourself at the feet of the priests; you must implore the intercession of the Church; you must try all means which may prevent your perishing everlastingly." And St. Ambrose says, in his second book of *Penance,* Chapter 10: "Can anyone imagine that he is doing penance while he is indulging his ambition in the pursuit of honors, while he is following wine, etc. The true penitent must renounce the world, must abridge even the necessary time of sleep, must interrupt it with his sighs and cut it short with his prayers." And St. Caesarius of Arles adds: "As often as we visit the sick, or those that are in prison, or reconcile together those that are at variance one with another; as often as we fast on days commanded by the Church, give alms to the poor that pass by our door, etc.—by these and suchlike works, our small sins are daily redeemed. But this alone is not enough for capital crimes; we must add tears and lamentations and long fasts, and give large alms, to the utmost of our power." (Homily 8). Thus, as the same Saint tells us, "By present mortification will be prevented the future sentence of eternal death. Thus, by humbling the guilty will the guilt be consumed; and by this voluntary severity, the wrath of a dreadful Judge will be appeased. These short penitential labors will pay off those vast debts, which otherwise everlasting burning would never have discharged." (Homily 1). Christians, let us follow in practice these excellent guides.

Chapter 22

Against Delay of Repentance

The Twenty-Second Day

CONSIDER FIRST that, of all the deceits of Satan by which he deludes poor sinners to their eternal ruin, there is none greater or more dangerous than this by which he persuades them to put off their repentance and conversion from time to time, till there is no more time for them. Alas! Thousands and millions of poor souls have been thus betrayed into everlasting flames, souls who never planned to damn themselves by dying in sin—any more than any one of us at present does. But, by putting off their conversion, they have, by a just judgment of God, been surprised by death when they least expected it; and dying as they lived, have been justly sentenced to that second and everlasting death. Unhappy wretches who would not believe their Just Judge, who in the Gospel so often warns them to watch and who declares to them that otherwise He will come at a time when they least expect Him! Ah, how dreadful and how common are these unprovided deaths!

Consider secondly the great presumption of sinners who put off their reconciliation with an offended God till another time, shutting their ears to His voice, by which He calls them at present, and refusing Him the entrance to their heart, where He stands and knocks. *"Behold, I stand at the gate and knock. If any man shall hear my*

*voice and open to me the door, I will come in to him, and
will sup with him, and he with me."*—(*Apocalypse* 3:20),
Alas! If He withdraw Himself, they are undone forever!
How dare they then treat Him with so much contempt! Is
it not an infinite goodness and an inexpressible conde-
scension in His Sovereign Majesty to call after them
when they are running from Him, and so earnestly to
press them, without any need on His part, to return to
Him who is their only Good and only Happiness? What
then ought they not to expect from His justice, if they
obstinately and insolently refuse to embrace His mercy?
How dare they pretend to dispose of the time to come, or
promise themselves greater graces thereafter than those
which they now abuse? Do they not know that God alone
is master of time and grace and that by His just judgment those who presume to tempt Him in this manner,
generally speaking, die in their sins? Ah, it is too true
that He who has promised pardon to the sinner who
repents sincerely, has promised neither time nor effica-
cious grace to those who defer their conversion. Quoting
Isaias (49:8), St. Paul says, *"In an accepted time have I
heard thee, and in the day of salvation have I helped thee.
Behold, now is the acceptable time; behold, now is the day
of salvation."* (*2 Corinthians* 6:2).

   Consider thirdly the great folly of sinners who put off
their conversion to God until another time, upon pre-
tense of doing it more easily hereafter; whereas, both reason and experience make it evident that the longer they
defer this work, the harder it is to bring it about. And
how can it be otherwise, since by this delay and by daily
adding sin to sin, their sinful habits grow daily stronger,
the devil's power over them increases, and God Almighty,
who is daily more and more provoked, by degrees is less
liberal of His graces, so that they become less frequent
and less pressing—till at length, by accustoming themselves to resist God's grace, they fall into the wretched
state of blindness and hardness of heart, the "broad road"
to final impenitence!

Consider fourthly the unparalleled madness of those who defer their conversion upon the confidence of a death-bed repentance, planning to cheat God's justice by indulging themselves in sin all their lifetime and then making their peace with God when they can sin no longer. Unhappy wretches, who will not consider that *"God is not mocked. For what things a man shall sow, those also shall he reap!"* (*Galatians* 6:7-8). The general rule is that, as a man lives, so he dies—a rule so general that, in the whole of Scripture, we have but one example of a person who died well after a wicked life, viz., that of the Good Thief, an example so singular in all its circumstances as to give no kind of encouragement to such sinners who entertain a premeditated design of escaping God's justice by a deathbed conversion. Ah! How dreadfully difficult must it be to a dying sinner, in whom the habit of sin has been by long custom turned into a second nature, to attain to that thorough change of heart, that sincere sorrow and detestation of sin above all evils and that love of God above all things, which he never thought of in his lifetime and which now, at least, are certainly necessary. Ah, how deceitful too often are those tears which are shed by dying sinners (as we see in the case of King Antiochus), which being wholly influenced by the fear of death, prevail not with the Just Judge! And if there be so much danger, even when tears are plentifully shed, what must there be when, as it commonly happens, either the dullness and stupidity caused by the sickness, or the pains and agonies of the body and mind are so great as to hinder any serious application of the thoughts to the greatest of all our concerns? For if a little headache be enough to hinder us from being able to pray with any devotion, what must be the agonies of death? No wonder, then, that the Saints and servants of God make so little account of these deathbed performances, especially since, as we see by daily experience, those who have made the greatest show of repentance when they were in danger of death have no sooner escaped that danger than they become the same men they were before.

O Christians, let us not then be imposed upon by the false and flattering discourses of men, who are so free in pronouncing favorably about all those who, after a life spent in sin, make some show of repentance at their death. Let us rather tremble at the deplorable case of such souls and remember that the judgments of God are very different from those of men.

Chapter 23

On Time and Eternity

The Twenty-Third Day

CONSIDER FIRST how precious a thing time is, which we are apt to squander away as if it were of no value. Time is the measure of life, and as much as we lose of our time, so much of our life is absolutely lost. All of our time is given to us in order to gain eternity, and there is not one moment of our time in which we may not work for eternity and in which we may not store up immense treasures for a happy eternity. As many, therefore, as we lose of these precious moments, they are so many lost eternities. This present time is the only time of working; it is the only time we can call our own, and only God knows how long it will be so. It is short, it flies away in an instant, and when once it is gone, it cannot be recalled. The very moment in which we are reading this line is now passing—never, never more to return. Every hour is slipping away, without stopping one moment, till it be swallowed up in the immense gulf of eternity; and as many of these hours or moments as are lost, are lost forever. The loss is irreparable! Learn hence, O my Soul, to set a just value upon thy present time; learn to use it well by employing it in good works.

Consider secondly, Christian Soul, what thy thoughts will be at the approach of death regarding the value of this time of which thou makest so little at present. What wouldst thou not give then for some of those hours which thou losest now in vanity and sin? Ah, the dreadful anguish that will rack the soul of the dying sinner when, seeing himself at the brink of a miserable eternity, he shall wish a thousand times, but all in vain, that he could call back one day, or even one hour, of his past time and had but the same health and strength as he formerly had to employ it in the love of God and sincere repentance for his sins! Ah, Worldlings, why will you then be so blind as not to see that any one of these hours which you daily squander away is indeed more valuable to you than ten thousand worlds!

Consider thirdly what will be the sentiments of the damned in Hell of the value of time, when time shall be no more! How bitterly will they regret, for all eternity, all those hours, days, months and years which were allowed them by the bounty of their Creator during the space of their mortal life, by the due employment of which they might have prevented that misery to which they are now irrevocably condemned and might have made themselves eternally and infinitely happy. But alas, they would not work while there was time, while they had the daylight before them. The night, the dismal and eternal night is now come, in which it is too late to work and during which they shall eternally condemn their past folly and madness in neglecting and abusing their precious time. Ah, Christians, let us be wise at their expense! But what do you think will be the sentiments of the Blessed in Heaven regarding this precious time? Truly, if it were possible, and if their happy state could admit of such a thing as grief, there is nothing that those Blessed Souls would regret more than the loss of any of those moments which, in their lifetime, had not been well husbanded, when they shall clearly see, in the light of God, what an immense increase of glory and happiness they might have acquired by the due employment of those precious moments.

Consider fourthly that, as all time is short and passes

quickly away, so all temporal enjoyments, honors, riches and pleasures of this world are all transitory, uncertain and inconstant. Only eternity, and the goods or evils which it comprises, are truly great, as being without end, without change, without comparison—admitting of no mixture of evil in the goods, or any allaying comfort in the evils. Oh, the vanity of all temporal grandeur, which must so soon be buried in the coffin! Oh, how quickly does the glory of this world pass away! A few short years are more than anyone can promise himself, and after that, Poor Sinner, what will become of thee? Alas, the worms will prey upon thy body, and merciless devils on thine unrepenting soul! Thy worldly friends will soon forget thee; the very stones on which thou hast thy name engraved will not long outlive thee! Oh, how true is that sentence, "*'Vanity of vanities, and all is vanity,'* but to love God and to serve him alone." (Thomas à Kempis, quoting *Ecclesiastes* 1:2). It is only thus that we shall be wise for eternity; all other wisdom is but folly.

Chapter 24

On the Presence of God

The Twenty-Fourth Day

CONSIDER FIRST that God is everywhere. *"If I ascend into heaven,"* says the Psalmist, *"thou art there; if I descend into hell, thou art there."* (*Psalm* 138:8). He fills both Heaven and earth, and there is no created thing whatsoever in which He is not truly and perfectly present. In Him we live, in Him we move, our very being is in Him. (*"For in him we live, and move, and are."—Acts of the Apostles* 17:28). As the birds, wherever they fly, meet with the air, which encompasses them on all sides; as the fishes swimming in the ocean everywhere meet with the waters; so we, wherever we are, or whithersoever we go, meet with God. We have Him always with us; He is more intimately present to our very souls than our souls are to our bodies. Alas, my Poor Soul, how little have we thought of this! And yet it is an article of our Faith, in which we have been instructed from the very cradle. Let us seriously reflect on this truth for the future; let us strive to be always with Him, who is always with us.

Consider secondly that God, being everywhere, sees us wherever we are; all our actions are done in His sight. Our very thoughts, even the most secret motions and dispositions of our hearts, cannot be concealed from His all-seeing eye. In vain does the sinner flatter himself in his crimes, like the libertine mentioned by the Wise Man: *"Darkness compasseth me about, and the walls cover me, and no man seeth me, whom do I fear? The most High will not remember my sins."* This sinner *"knoweth not that the eyes of the Lord are infinitely brighter than the rays of the sun,"* (*Ecclesiasticus* 23:26, 28), and no darkness, no clouds, no walls or curtains can keep out His piercing sight, which clearly sees the very center of the soul. And no wonder that He should clearly see what passes there, where He is always present.

Consider thirdly that God, who is in all places and in all things, is everywhere whole and entire, because He is indivisible. He is everywhere with all His Majesty, with all His attributes, with all His perfections. We have then within us, my Soul, the eternal, immense, omnipotent, self-existent, infinite Lord and Maker of all things, and we are within this Infinite Being. Wherever we are, we have Him with us. He is everywhere with His omnipotence, to which all things are subject. What then have His friends to fear? He is everywhere with His infinite justice; how then can His enemies be secure? He is everywhere infinitely good to His children; His love and kindness to them surpass those of the most tender mother. He watches over them with His providence; His wisdom wonderfully disposes all things for their greater good. What comfort then must this thought of the presence of God afford His servants and those who truly fear and love Him!

Consider fourthly that God, being everywhere, requires of us that we should everywhere take notice of His presence. Can there be an object more worthy of our attention? And shall we then be so unfortunately blind as to amuse ourselves about every trifle that comes our way, and let our God, the Sovereign Beauty and the Sovereign Good, pass unregarded? Ah, let us never regret our being alone, since we always have in our company that Infinite Being, the sight and enjoyment of whom are the eternal felicity of the Angels! What if we do not see Him with the eyes of the body? Is He the less present? And, have we not within us other more noble eyes, that is, the eyes of the understanding, which, assisted by divine faith, may and ought to contemplate their God always present in the very midst of us? Ah, the sweetest repose is to be found in Him! All other recreations are vain compared to this.

Consider fifthly that God, being everywhere present, requires of us that we should compose ourselves, both as to the interior and exterior, in such manner as becomes those who are standing in His sight. The presence of a person for whom we have respect is enough to put a restraint upon us from doing anything that is light and indecent—and shall not the infinite majesty of God, in comparison with whom the greatest monarchs of the earth are less than nothing, keep us by His presence in that exterior modesty and interior reverence which may please His eyes? Ought we not even to annihilate ourselves in the sight of this Immense Divinity? But, O Good God, how far we are from these dispositions as often as we dare to sin in Thine Almighty Presence and fly in the face of Thy Sovereign Majesty! Alas, my Poor Soul, how we would be ashamed to have our sins known to persons whose esteem we covet! We would be ready even to die with humiliation rather than to have them published to the whole world. We would be very unwilling to have even our vain and ridiculous amusements, though otherwise innocent, laid open to the eyes of our neighbors. And why will we not consider the all-seeing eye of our great God, which is always upon us, which clearly discerns all that passes in the most secret closet of our heart? Why will we not reflect that our evil thoughts, being known to God, is indeed a greater shame, a greater loss of our true honor, than if they were published by sound of trumpet over the universe?

Consider sixthly that God, being everywhere present, everywhere requires our love. He is everywhere infinitely amiable, infinitely beautiful, infinitely good, infinitely perfect; and wherever we are, He is infinitely good to us. Why then do we not love Him? He is all love: *"Deus charitas est,"* says St. John—*"God is love!"* (*1 John* 4:8, 16). We have this loving and most lovely God always with us and always in us. Why do we not run to His embraces? He is a fire that ever burns; this fire is in the very center of our souls; how is it that we feel so little of its flames? It is because we will not stand by it. It is because we will not keep our souls at home—attentive to that Great Guest who resides within us—but let them continually wander abroad upon vain created amusements. *"Turn, O my soul, into thy rest."* (*Psalm* 114:7). Turn away from all these worldly toys which keep thee from thy God, and return to Him—thy True and Only Happiness—and in Him repose forever.

Chapter 25

On the Passion of Christ: and First, on Our Saviour in the Garden of Gethsemane

The Twenty-Fifth Day

CONSIDER FIRST how the Son of God—who came down from Heaven and clothed Himself with our humanity in order to be our priest and our victim and to offer Himself as a bleeding sacrifice to His Eternal Father for our sins—was pleased to begin His Passion by a bloody sweat and agony in the Garden of Gethsemane the night before His death. Here, having left the rest of His disciples at some distance and taking with Him Peter, James and John, who before had been witnesses of His glorious Transfiguration on Mount Thabor, He begins to disclose to them that mortal anguish, fear and sadness which oppressed His heart. *"My soul,"* saith He, *"is sorrowful even unto death,"* (*Matthew* 26:38), that is, with a sadness which even now would strike Me dead if I did not preserve Myself, in order to suffer still more for you. Sweet Jesus, what can be the meaning of this? Didst Thou not lately cry out, speaking of Thy Passion and the desire that Thou hadst of suffering for us: *"I have a baptism, wherewith I am to be baptised, and how am I straitened until it be accomplished?"* (*Luke* 12:50). Whence then comes this present sadness? Was it not Thou who hast given that strength and courage to Thy martyrs, as not even to shrink under the worst of torments? And art Thou Thyself afraid? But, O Dear Lord, I plainly understand that it was by Thine own choice that Thou hadst condescended so far as to let Thyself be seized with this mortal anguish. It was for my instruction and that Thou might suffer so much the more for me. I adore Thee under this weakness—if I may be allowed to call it so— no less than on Thy throne of glory, because it is here that I better discover Thine infinite love for me.

Consider secondly how our dear Saviour, under this anguish and sadness, betakes Himself to prayer, the only sure refuge under all afflictions, the only shield in the day of battle. But take notice, my Soul, with what reverence He prays to His Eternal Father, prostrate on the very ground: with what fervor, *"with a strong cry and tears,"* says the Apostle (*Hebrews* 5:7), and learn to imitate Him. In this prayer He condescended so far as to allow the inferior part of His soul to petition that the cup of His bitter Passion might be removed from Him. But then He immediately added, *"Yet not my will, but thine be done,"* (*Luke* 22:42), to teach us, under all trials and crosses, a perfect submission and resignation to the Divine Will.

Consider thirdly how our Saviour made two interruptions in His prayers to come and visit His disciples, but found them both times asleep. Ah, my Soul, is it not thy case, like these Apostles, to sleep—that is, to indulge thyself in a slothful, sensual way of living; whereas, the whole life of thy Saviour was spent in laboring for thy salvation? And all that He now suffers He suffers for thee. Ah, pity now at least His comfortless condition, while on the one hand, His Father seems deaf to His prayers, and on the other hand, His disciples are too drowsy to give any attention to Him. In this desolate state, an Angel from Heaven appears to comfort Him, who is Himself the Joy of the Angels. Oh, what humility!

But what kind of comfort, think you, did this Angel bring? None other but the representing to Him the Will of His Eternal Father and humbly entreating Him, in the name of Heaven and earth, not to decline the imparting to poor sinners by His infinite love of that plentiful Redemption for which He came into the world, and to undergo the ignominies and torments of one short day's duration in the prospect of the salvation of mankind and of that eternal glory and honor which the Godhead would receive from all His sufferings. Let the like consideration of God's will, His greater honor and glory, and the good of thine own soul comfort thee also under all thine anguish and crosses. There can be no comfort more solid.

Consider fourthly the mortal agony which our Saviour suffered in His soul during the prayer of this night. We may judge the pains and anguish of His soul by the astonishing effect which they produced in His body, by casting Him into that prodigious sweat of blood to such a degree as to stain the very ground on which He lay prostrate. Sweet Jesus, who ever heard of such an agony as this? But what thinkest thou, my Soul, were the true causes of all this anguish and of this bitter Agony of thy Saviour? Chiefly these three: *First,* a clear view and lively representation of all that He was to suffer during the whole course of His Passion, so that all the ignominies and torments that He was afterwards successively to go through were now all at once presented before the eyes of His soul, with all their respective aggravations, by means of which He suffered His whole bitter Passion twice over—once by the hands of His enemies, and another time by His own most clear and lively imagination of all that He had to suffer. But why, Dear Jesus, these additional agonies? Only Thy love can answer me.

A *second* cause that contributed to our Saviour's anguish was a distinct view of all the sins of the world, from the first to the last: of all the horrid crimes and abominations of mankind, all now laid to His charge, to be cancelled by the last drop of His blood. Ah, how hideous, how detestable were all these hellish monsters in the eyes of our Saviour, who alone had a just notion of their enormity by having always before Him a clear sight of the Infinite Majesty offended by them! O Lord, how great a share had *my* sins in this tragic scene! How much, alas, did *they* contribute to Thy pains and grief!

A *third* cause of our Saviour's Agony was the fore-knowledge He had of the little use that even Christians would make of all His sufferings, and of the eternal loss of so many millions of souls for whom He was to die—of the blindness and hardness of heart by which they would pervert this antidote into a mortal poison and tread under their feet His Precious Blood! All these sad and melancholy thoughts, attacking at once the soul of our Redeemer, cast Him into that mortal Agony and forced from Him those streams of blood. O Christians, pity now thy Saviour's anguish, and resolve never more to have any hand in afflicting His tender soul by sin.

Chapter 26

On Our Saviour in the Court Of Caiphas

The Twenty-Sixth Day

CONSIDER FIRST how our Saviour, arising from His prayer, having conquered all His fears, comes to His disciples, bidding them now to sleep on and take their rest, adding that His hour was now come and that the traitor was at hand. But Thou, Dear Lord, when wilt *Thou* rest or sleep? Not till the last sleep of death on the hard bed of the Cross. O Christians, contemplate with the eyes of your souls the courage and readiness to suffer for you which your Saviour shows on this occasion by going forth to meet the traitor and his band. See with what meekness He receives the treacherous kiss of peace. And yet, to make it evident that no power upon earth could take Him except of His own free will, with two words, *Ego sum*—"I am he," *(John* 18:5), He struck down the whole multitude that was come to apprehend Him, making them all reel back and fall to the ground. After this, He delivered Himself into their hands; and they, having bound Him, dragged Him along into the city, through thick and thin, while all His disciples, abandoning Him, ran their way, leaving Him in the hands of His enemies, who presented Him first before Annas, the father-in-law of the High Priest, where He was insulted by a servant, who gave Him a box on the ear. Thence they led Him to the court of Caiphas, where the chief priests and elders were assembled, longing to see this new prisoner before them and determined to do away with Him, right or wrong. Follow thou thy Saviour, my Soul, every step of the way, abandoned now by all His friends. Contemplate this meek Lamb in the midst of these ravenous wolves, loaded with their scoffs and insolence. But carry the eyes of thy understanding still further; view the interior of His soul, and see the joy and satisfaction that He takes in complying with His Eternal Father's will and in suffering for thee, and from this learn to have similar dispositions in all thy sufferings.

Consider secondly how Our Lord was no sooner brought to the court of Caiphas, the High Priest, where the great council of the Sanhedrin was assembled, than immediately after a scornful welcome, they proceed to His trial and to call in the false witnesses who were to depose against Him. But see the providence of God; see the force of truth and the wonderful innocence of this Lamb of God: notwithstanding all the malice of this impious court and their witnesses—men neither of honor nor of conscience—yet all that they could allege against Him was either insignificant, or they could not agree in their story, which made their testimonies of no weight. But while thou dost adore this Providence, see and admire the meekness and patience of thy Saviour, who was silent under all the provocations from these false witnesses, giving thereby a most convincing proof of His being something more than man, since He could calmly hold His peace while His reputation and His life were both attacked by obvious calumnies. The malice of our Saviour's enemies being thus confounded, the High Priest arises and adjures Him by the living God to tell him if He be the CHRIST, the SON of GOD! In reverence to this adorable name, Our Lord made a solemn confession and profession of the truth, teaching by His example all His followers, when put to a similar test, never to be ashamed of Him or of His Faith. Upon this, Caiphas rends his garments, crying out, *"Blasphemy!"* (Cf. *Mark* 14:63-64). And they all pronounce Him worthy of death. But thou, my Soul, on the contrary, cry out with the Angels and all the elect of God: *"The Lamb that was slain is worthy to receive power, and divinity, and wisdom, and strength, and honour, and glory, and benediction"* from all creatures forever and ever. (*Apocalypse* 5:12-13).

Consider thirdly how that unjust sentence against our Redeemer was no sooner pronounced by the great council than immediately they all, with unheard-of barbarity, fell upon Him like furies of Hell rather than men, and discharged upon Him all kinds of injuries, blows, affronts and blasphemies! See, my Soul, how they spit in thy Saviour's face and disgorge their filthy phlegm on that sacred forehead, where Beauty and Majesty sit. See how they buffet, kick and strike Him with merciless rage, while He, with His hands tied behind Him, is not able to ward off even one blow, nor has He any friend to wipe His face or afford Him any help. See how they cover and muffle up His face with some filthy rag, and then in scorn, as if He were a mock-prophet and an imposter, at every blow bid Him prophesy who it was that struck Him, besides many other affronts—which He endured with an invincible patience and fortitude.

Consider fourthly that, of all which our Saviour suffered in the court of Caiphas, nothing touched Him so much to the quick as the dangerous fall of Peter, the chief of all His Apostles and the one who had received the most signal favors from Him: Peter, who, after having boasted that very night that although all the rest of the disciples might abandon their Master, he would never forsake Him and that he would rather die with Him than deny Him. Yet at the voice of a servant maid (see the weakness and inconstancy of human nature), he forthwith denies his Master, repeats this denial a second and a third time, and even swears and curses himself if he ever knew the man.

Sweet Jesus! What is man? O Lord, look to me and support me by Thy grace, or I shall also deny Thee. The causes of Peter's fall were, *first,* a secret pride and presumption upon his own strength; *secondly,* his neglect of the admonition of our Saviour by sleeping when he ought to have watched and prayed; *thirdly,* his exposing himself to the danger by running into bad company. See that the same causes do not have the same effect on thee, by drawing thee also to deny, and even to crucify thy Lord by sin. Learn to imitate the speedy repentance of this Apostle, who immediately after his fall, going out, wept bitterly—a practice which it is said he ever after retained as often as he heard a cock crow.

Consider fifthly how the High Priest and scribes, after having given sentence of death against our Saviour, retired to take their rest, leaving Him in hands that were not likely to allow Him to take any rest. Oh, what a night did Our Lord pass in the midst of that rabble, who to satisfy their own cruelty and the malice of their masters, acted over and over again all that scene of inhumanity which they had begun while their masters were there, and loaded Him with all kinds of outrage and blasphemies, so that we may boldly affirm that one-half of what our Saviour suffered that night will not be known till the Day of Judgment. All these insolences He bears in silence—and even then, while they are abusing Him, He is praying for them and excusing them to His Father and offering up all His sufferings in atonement for their sins. Sweet Jesus, give us the grace to imitate Thee!

Chapter 27

Our Saviour Is Brought before Pilate and Herod

The Twenty-Seventh Day

CONSIDER FIRST how, early in the morning, notwithstanding their late sitting up, the High Priest and his fellows in iniquity convene a more numerous assembly of the Sanhedrin and there again put the same question to our Saviour—*"Art thou then the Son of God?" (Luke* 22:70)—and receiving the same answer, confirm their former sentence. Yet, as they did not think it safe for themselves, being subject to the Roman Empire, to put this sentence into execution without the consent of Pontius Pilate, the governor, they determined to carry Him to Pilate and by Pilate's authority to have Him crucified—a kind of execution of which their malice made choice because it was at the same time the most ignominious, as being only for vile slaves and notorious criminals, and the most cruel, as being a long and lingering death, under the sharpest and most excruciating torments. Come now, Christian Soul, and contemplate thy Saviour as He is hurried along the streets with His hands bound, from the house of the High Priest to the court of Pilate, accompanied by the whole Council and their wicked ministers, proclaiming aloud as they go that now all His impostures were laid open, His hypocrisy revealed and Himself convicted of blasphemy. See how the giddy mob, who a little while before reverenced Him as a Prophet, now all of a sudden join with His enemies, following Him with opprobrious shouts, insulting Him all the way that He goes and discharging a thousand kinds of injuries and insults upon Him.

Consider secondly, and view the Judge of the Living and the Dead, standing with His hands bound as a criminal before a petty governor, and behold the process. The chief priests and princes of the people having delivered Him up and Pilate demanding what particulars they had to allege against Him, they made no scruple of inventing new calumnies—that He was a factious and seditious man, a traitor and a rebel to the government, that He forbade tribute to be paid to Caesar and set Himself up as the King of the Jews. Once more take notice of the invincible patience of thy Saviour in hearing in silence such notorious falsities as they laid to His charge, so that the governor was astonished that a man could hold His peace under such accusations, which aimed at nothing less than procuring His condemnation to the worst of deaths. However, as he plainly saw through all the disguise of the High Priest and Scribes, he interpreted this silence in favor of our Saviour, but boggling a little at the word *"king,"* and having received full satisfaction upon that score by being made to understand that the kingdom of Our Saviour was not of this world and therefore not dangerous to Caesar's government, he determined to set Him at liberty. Admire the force of innocence which could move even a heathen, and one of the worst of men, such as Pilate was, and assure thyself that, generally speaking, patience and silence are a thousand times better proofs of thy innocence than returning injury for injury and making an opprobrious and clamorous defense.

Consider thirdly how Pilate, being convinced of our Saviour's innocence and desirous of setting Him at liberty, met with an obstinate resistance from the malicious priests and deluded people, and therefore understanding

that our Saviour, being an inhabitant of Galilee, belonged
to the jurisdiction of Herod, the tetrarch of Galilee, he
took occasion to rid himself of their importunity by send-
ing Him to Herod. Accompany thy Lord, O my Soul, in
this new stage, and take notice of His incomparable
meekness while He passes through the streets, lined on
all sides with an insulting multitude and echoing with
their reproaches and clamors. Herod was most glad of
His coming, in hopes of seeing some miracle, and therefore put a thousand questions to Him—while the priests
of the Jews, with untired malice, were repeating all their
false accusations against Him. But Our Lord was still
silent, nor would He satisfy the curiosity of Herod or do
anything by which He might incline this prince to free
Him from that death which He so ardently desired, as
being by the decrees of Heaven the only means of our
Redemption. Blessed by all His creatures be His goodness forever!

Consider fourthly how Herod, provoked by our Saviour's not consenting to gratify his desire of seeing a miracle, sought to revenge himself by treating Him with
mockery and scorn, exposing Him to the scoffs of all his
guards and, in contempt, ordering Him to be clothed in a
white garment, as with a fool's coat, or perhaps as a mock
king, and in this dress sent Him back again to Pilate,
accompanied in the same manner as He came—with an
insulting mob headed by the Scribes and Pharisees.
Stand amazed, my Soul, to see the Wisdom of the Eternal
Father treated thus as a fool, and learn from this not to
fret over at or be solicitous about the judgment of the
world.

Consider fifthly how Pilate, seeing our Saviour
brought back again to the Tribunal, contrived another
way to get Him off, in order at the same time to give as
little offense as possible to the High Priest and to the
chiefs of the Jews. It was the custom of that nation, on
the day of their Paschal solemnity—which was celebrated that very day in memory of their delivery from the

Egyptian bondage—to have one criminal set at liberty for whom the people would petition. Wherefore, Pilate, taking advantage of this opportunity, proposed to their choice our Saviour, on the one hand, and Barabbas, a notorious malefactor, robber and murderer, on the other—making sure that they would rather choose to have released the innocent Lamb of God than have Barabbas, the worst of all criminals, escape due punishment. Ah, Pilate, what an outrageous affront dost thou thus offer to the Son of God, while thou dost pretend to favor Him! What? Must the Lord of Life and Immortality, the King of Heaven, stand in competition with the vilest of men, with the most notorious criminal that could be suggested? Must it be put to the vote of the mob which of the two is the better man and which is the more worthy of death? Oh, the unparalleled injury! Oh, the unparalleled humility of my Saviour! O King of Glory, how low hast Thou stooped to raise me up from the dunghill!

Consider sixthly, if it was an intolerable affront to compare our Saviour with Barabbas, what idea must we frame—or what name must we give—to that blind people's choice when they preferred Barabbas to Christ and desired that the latter might be crucified and the former acquitted! O my Soul, see in this astonishing humiliation of thy Lord how deep, how dangerous was the wound of pride which could not be cured but by such and so great a humility! Oh, see if thine be yet cured! Examine thyself also if thou hast not often been guilty, like these blind Jews, of preferring Barabbas to your Saviour, by turning thy back on Him for some petty interest or filthy pleasure. If so, thou art more inexcusable than they, because thou knowest Him to be the Lord of Glory at the same time that thou dost persecute Him by sin; whereas, if they had known Him to be so, they would never have preferred a Barabbas before Him.

Chapter 28

Our Saviour Is Scourged at the Pillar and Crowned with Thorns

The Twenty-Eighth Day

CONSIDER FIRST how the Jews were still continuing to cry out against Our Lord and in a tumultuous manner to demand His crucifixion. Pilate then takes another way to bring about His being set at liberty, which was by striving to satisfy their cruelty in ordering Him to be most severely scourged. O Pilate, how cruel is thy mercy! Is it thus that thou dost treat Him whom thou dost declare innocent? Is this thy justice? But our sins, O my Soul, required that the Lord of Glory should be thus cruelly treated and subjected to this ignominious punishment, to which none but common slaves or the meanest wretches were liable and to which a Roman citizen could on no account be condemned. Stand thou and see, my Soul, in what manner this sentence is executed. See how the bloody soldiers lay hands on the Lamb of God, how they strip Him of all His clothes and tie Him fast to a stony pillar. See how they discharge upon His sacred back and shoulders innumerable stripes, lashes and scourges. See how the blood comes spouting forth on all sides. See how His body is all rent and mangled by their cruelty and the flesh laid open to the very bones. See how His enemies are all the while insulting Him and rejoicing at His torments, while He, with His eyes turned up toward Heaven, is offering up all that He suffers for their sins and for those of the whole world. Ah, Sinners, take a serious view of your Redeemer now, and see in His torn and mangled body the malice of sin; and learn to detest this hellish monster, which has brought the Son of God to all these sufferings!

Consider secondly how these bloody ruffians, having by this cruel scourging made our Saviour's body one wound from head to foot, loose Him at last from the pillar, leaving Him to help Himself on with His clothes as well as He can. Ah, Christians, pity now your Saviour's abandoned condition, who has no one to lend Him a helping hand, to bind up His gaping wounds, or to staunch the blood that comes flowing from them! Oh, present yourselves now and offer Him what services you are able; offer at least to assist Him in putting on His clothes, to cover His open wounds from the cold air! But oh, how rough are these woolen clothes to His wounded back! Alas! Instead of affording Him any ease or comfort, they do but increase His wounds by rubbing upon them.

Consider thirdly how the bloody soldiers had scarcely given our Saviour a short respite after His scourging when they were pushed on by the devil to act another scene of cruelty such as was never heard of before or since, and that was to make themselves a barbarous sport in crowning Him as a king. Therefore, they drag Him into the court of the Praetorium and assemble together the whole regiment; then violently they strip Him again of all His clothes—which now begin to cleave to His wounded body—set Him on a bench or stool, throw about Him some old ragged purple garment, twist a wreath of long, hard and sharp thorns, and press it down on His sacred head. They put in His hand for a scepter, a reed or cane; then in derision, coming one by one, they bend their knees before Him with a scornful salutation: *"Hail, king of the Jews."* (*Matthew* 27:29). They spit in His face, buffet Him and, taking the reed or cane out of His hand, strike Him with it on the head, thus driving the thorns in deeper, while the blood trickles down swiftly from the many wounds which He receives from their points. Sweet Jesus, what shall we say here, or which shall we marvel at more: the malice of these ministers of Satan or Thine unparalleled charity, which made Thee undergo such unheard-of reproaches and torments for ungrateful sinners? Blessed by all creatures be Thy goodness forever!

Consider fourthly how Pilate—hoping now that the rage and malice of the Jews would be satisfied so that they would insist no longer upon our Saviour's death after they would see with how much cruelty and contempt He had been treated in compliance with their fury—leads Him forth as He was, with His crown of thorns on His head and His ragged purple on His shoulders; and from an eminence Pilate shows Him to the people with the words, *Ecce homo—"Behold the Man!" (John* 19:5). It is as if Pilate said: "Behold in what manner He has now been treated; cease then to seek His death any longer. Let His body, mangled from head to foot, beseech your pity." But thou, Christian Soul, *"Behold the Man"* with other eyes than those of these hard-hearted wretches, and see to what a condition thy sins and His own infinite charity have reduced Him. Behold His head, crowned with a wreath of sharp thorns, piercing on all sides His sacred flesh and entering into His temples with excessive pain. Behold His face, quite disfigured, black and blue with bruises, and all besmeared with spittle and blood. Behold His whole body, inhumanly rent and torn with whips and scourges, and now covered with a hard ragged garment which is rubbing and at each moment increasing His wounds. And then look up and contemplate Him upon His Throne of Glory, and see what return thou canst make to Him for having thus annihilated Himself for the love of thee. He desires no more of thee than an imitation of His patience and humility. See then in what manner thou art to practice these lessons.

Chapter 29

Our Saviour Carries His Cross, And Is Nailed to It

The Twenty-Ninth Day

CONSIDER FIRST how—the malice of the Jews in no way relenting at the sight of the Lamb of God bleeding for the sins of the world, but continuing still in a tumultuous manner to demand that He might be crucified—Pilate at last yields to their importunity and against his own conscience sentences Our Saviour to the death of the cross. Ah, Christians, has it never been your misfortune by a similar cowardice to condemn our Saviour and His doctrine and basely to renounce in the practice of your lives the maxims of His Gospel for fear of what the world might say? Has not too often a much weaker temptation than the fear of losing Caesar's friendship induced you to crucify again the Son of God? Be confounded and repent!

Consider secondly how this sentence of death—however unjust from Pilate, yet as being most just from His Eternal Father and necessary for our salvation—was received with perfect submission, charity and silence by our Redeemer, who thereupon was immediately stripped again of His purple garment and clad with His own clothes, and a heavy cross, of length and size proportionate to the bearing of a man, was laid upon His wounded shoulders. And two thieves, or highway robbers, were appointed to bear Him company and to be executed with Him, to verify that prophecy, He *"was reputed with the wicked."* (*Isaias* 53:12). Come now, Devout Souls, and consider Our Lord in this His last procession. A crier leads the way, publishing aloud the pretended crimes and blasphemies of this unheard-of malefactor; then follow the soldiers and executioners with ropes, hammers, nails, etc. After these goes, or rather, creeps along our High Priest and Victim, all bruised and bloody, with a thief on each hand and the Cross on His shoulders, dragging it forward step by step, followed and surrounded on all sides by the priests, the Scribes and the whole mob of the people, cursing, reviling and scoffing at Him, while the cruel executioners are hastening Him forward with their kicks and blows. Ah, Christians, now at least take pity on thy Saviour's sufferings and add not to His load by sin!

Consider thirdly how Our Blessed Lord, having for some time, with unspeakable labor and torment, carried His Cross through the streets, at last falls down under the weight, unable to carry it any farther. Wonder not, my Soul, at this, since besides the load of the Cross, which oppressed His wearied body, wounded in every part and exhausted by the loss of so much blood, His Heavenly Father has laid upon His shoulders another and more insupportable weight, namely that of the sins of the whole world. Ah, Christians, it is under this intolerable burden that your Saviour faints and falls down! Nor is He in any way eased of this merciless load by Simon of Cyrene, who was compelled to take up the Cross, but bore no part of the weight of our iniquities— all, of which the Heavenly Father laid upon His beloved Son, to be cancelled by His blood and death. O Infinite Goodness of the Father! O Infinite Charity of the Son! To do and to suffer so much for wretched man! O my Soul, see that thou nevermore be ungrateful to so loving a God.

Consider fourthly how our Saviour, being now arrived at Mount Calvary quite wearied and spent, the ministers of Hell still persecute Him with unwearied cruelty. And, whereas it was the custom to give to criminals that were to die a strengthening draught of wine seasoned with myrrh, they contrived to mingle gall with the portion prepared for Him. After this, they violently strip Him of all His clothes, which by this time clove fast to His sores, opening again all His wounds and exposing Him naked to shame and the cold in the sight of an immense multitude. Draw near now, my Soul, and see Him bleeding afresh for the love of thee. Oh see how, while the Cross is prepared, He falls upon His knees and offers Himself to His Eternal Father, a bleeding Victim to appease His wrath, enkindled by thy sins!

Consider fifthly how, the Cross lying flat on the ground, they lay our dear Redeemer stretched out upon it, who like a meek lamb, makes no resistance. And first drawing His right hand to the place prepared to fix it on, they drive with their hammers a sharp, gross nail through the palm, forcing its way with incredible torment through the sinews, veins, muscles and bones of which the hand is composed, into the hard wood of the Cross. In the meantime, the whole body, to favor that wound and the pierced sinews, was naturally drawn toward the right side, but it was not long permitted to remain so. For immediately these cruel butchers, laying hold of His other arm and hand, violently drag Him toward the left side, in order to nail that hand also to the place prepared for it. Then pulling down His legs, they fasten His sacred feet, in like manner, with nails to the wood. And all this is done with such violent cruelty that it is thought, with stretching and pulling, they very much strained His whole body and disjointed it in many parts, according to that saying of the Royal Prophet: *"They have dug my hands and feet. They have numbered all my bones."* (*Psalm* 21:17-18). Ah, Christians, if the contracting or piercing of any one nerve or sinew, if the disjointing or displacing of any one bone, ever so small, be so cruel a torture, what must we think of the torments which our

Saviour endured in His disjointed body! What must we think of what He suffered when His hands and feet—where so many sinews, muscles, veins and bones all meet—were violently bored through with gross nails! Oh, let us never forget His sufferings! Oh, let us never cease to admire, adore and love His mercy!

Chapter 30

Our Saviour on the Cross

The Thirtieth Day

CONSIDER FIRST how the bloody executioners, having now nailed Our Saviour fast to the Cross, begin with ropes to raise Him up in the air. Oh, what shouts did His enemies now make when He appeared above the people's heads! With what blasphemies did they salute Him, while His most afflicted Mother and other devout friends are pierced to the heart at the sight! At length they let the foot of the Cross fall with a jolt into the hole prepared for it, by which our Saviour's mangled body was not a little injured and the wounds of His hands and feet widened. And thus He now hangs, poised in the air, in most dreadful pangs and torments, the whole weight of His body sustained by His pierced hands and feet, by which His wounds are continually increased. There is no place to rest His head but upon thorns; no other bed for His wearied and wounded body but the hard wood of the Cross.

Consider secondly the infinite charity of our Saviour and the unparalleled malice of His enemies. He, amidst His torments, cries out, *"Father, forgive them, for they know not what they do." (Luke* 23:34). They grin and shake their heads at Him, saying, *"Vah! Thou that destroyest the temple of God and in three days dost rebuild it, save thy own self; if thou be the Son of God, come down from the cross."* (*Matthew* 27:40). With a thousand such other reproaches and blasphemies is He loaded, not only by the common people and soldiers, but also by the chief priests, Scribes and elders, which He hears in patience and silence. But oh, who can tell us the interior employment of His blessed Soul all this time that He hangs upon the Cross: His thoughts of peace toward us, His prayer for us, the anguish and dreadful agonies of the inferior part of His Soul, and the inexpressible joy in the superior part thereof in the glory of His Father, which was to arise from that plentiful Redemption which He was then imparting to poor sinners!

Consider thirdly that part that the Blessed Virgin Mother bore in the sufferings of her Son and how truly was here verified that prophecy of the aged Simeon: *"And thy own soul a sword shall pierce."* (*Luke* 2:35). Oh, how killing a grief must have oppressed this most tender and most loving of all mothers when—during the whole course of the Passion of her dearest Son, whom she loved with an incomparable love—she was an eyewitness to all the injuries, outrages and torments that He endured. Ah, Blessed Lady, may we not truly say that the whips, thorns and nails that pierced thy Son's flesh made so deep a wound in thy virginal heart that nothing but a miracle could have supported thy life under such excess of pain? But oh, what a deep wound didst thou feel in thy soul when thy dying Son recommended thee to His Beloved Disciple St. John, giving to thee the son of Zebedee in exchange for the Son of God! Blessed Virgin, we gladly acknowledge thee for our Mother, bequeathed to us all in the person of St. John. Oh, by all thy sufferings, remember us poor banished children of Eve before the Throne of Grace! Christians, learn the admirable lessons which Our Lady teaches you at the foot of the Cross. Learn her unshaken faith and undoubted hope. Learn her perfect resignation, patience and fortitude! Oh, learn from her to love Jesus and detest sin, the true cause of all His sufferings!

Consider fourthly how all things seem now to have conspired against our dearest Lord. His Father has forsaken Him; His mother's presence and grief pierce Him to the heart. As for His own Apostles, one of them has betrayed Him; another has denied Him; all, save one, have abandoned Him. His friends and those whom He had most favored and miraculously cured now either join with His persecutors, or at least are ashamed of Him. His enemies insult and triumph over Him. His own body, by its weight, is a torment to Him. But what most of all afflicts Him is the ingratitude of Christians and the little benefit which they will derive from His Passion and Death and the eternal loss of so many souls redeemed by His Precious Blood! Ah, Sweet Jesus, allow me not to be one of that unhappy number; allow me not to be so miserable as to join with Thine enemies in crucifying Thee by sin!

Consider fifthly the lessons that our Saviour gives us by His last words upon the Cross. *First* is perfect love and charity to His enemies by praying for them and excusing them to His eternal Father: *"Father, forgive them, for they know not what they do." (Luke* 23:34). Oh, let us learn from our dying Redeemer this necessary lesson, to love and pray for those that hate and persecute us, and instead of aggravating their crime, to excuse it and impute it to their ignorance! Oh, how true is it of every sinner: he knows not what he is doing; otherwise, he would never dare to fly in the face of Infinite Majesty; he would never be so mad as to renounce Heaven for a trifle and cast himself down the precipice that leads to Hell. *Secondly,* learn the efficacy of a sincere conversion and a humble confession of sin from the plenary indulgence given by our dying Saviour to the Good Thief. *"Amen, I say to thee, this day thou shalt be with me in Paradise." (Luke* 23:43). *Thirdly,* learn filial devotion to the Virgin Mother, commended to us all by her Son in the person of St. John: *"Behold thy mother." (John* 19:27). *Fourthly,* learn the greatness of the interior anguish of our Saviour's soul from those words: *"My God, my God, why hast thou forsaken me?"* (*Matthew* 27:46). Alas, it was for no other reason than that poor sinful man might not be forsaken! *Fifthly,* from those words of thy crucified Jesus, *"I thirst,"* (*John* 19:28), take notice of two violent thirsts which thy Saviour endured upon the Cross: the one corporal, proceeding from His having fasted so long, passed through so many torments and shed so much blood; the other spiritual, in His soul, by the vehement desire for our good and salvation. But oh, the cruel wretches who would give Him nothing but vinegar to quench His corporal thirst! But crueler sinners still are those who—instead of satisfying His spiritual thirst by gratitude and devotion—give Him nothing but the gall and vinegar of sin and wickedness! *Sixthly,* from these words of our dying Saviour, *"It is consummated,"* (*John* 19:30), learn to rejoice that the whole work of man's Redemption is now perfected, that the figures and prophecies of the Law are all fulfilled, and the handwriting that stood against us is now completely cancelled by the blood of our Redeemer. *Seventhly,* from those last words of our expiring Lord, *"Father, into thy hands I commend my spirit,"* (*Luke* 23:46), learn both in life and in death to commit thyself wholly to thy God. Happy they who study well these lessons which their great Master teaches them from the chair of His Cross.

Chapter 31

On the Death of Our Saviour

The Thirty-First Day

CONSIDER FIRST how Our Lord, having spoken these last words, *"Father, into thy hands I commend my spirit,"* (*Luke* 23:46), with a loud and strong voice, leaning down His head, in perfect submission to His Father's will and perfect charity to us poor sinners—to whom in this posture He offered, as it were, the kiss of peace—breathed forth His pure soul and thus ended His mortal life, which from the very first moment till now had been nothing but a series of sufferings endured for us. Run in now, my Soul, and approach boldly thy Redeemer: kiss His sacred feet, view His pale limbs, count at leisure all His wounds, and lament thy sins for which He suffered them all.

Consider secondly in the Passion of our Saviour the truth of those words, which He Himself delivered upon another occasion: *"He that shall humble himself shall be exalted,"* (*Matthew* 23:12), and see how Our Lord, having humbled Himself to the death of the Cross, was even at that very time honored and exalted by His Heavenly Father—and that in many ways. For during the time that He was upon the Cross, the sun for three whole hours withdrew its light; and at His death, the earth trembled, the rocks were split, and the tombs were opened; the veil of the Temple, which hung before the Sanctuary, was rent

111

from top to bottom. The people, touched with these wonders, went home striking their breasts; and the centurion, or captain of the guards, publicly professed that this man whom they had crucified was truly the Son of God! Rejoice, Christian Soul, to see thy Saviour's death thus honored, and learn under all circumstances to confide in God, who will make all the malice of thine enemies turn at last to thine honor and advantage. Sit down now at the foot of the Cross, and there at leisure

Consider Thirdly and repeat in thy mind the multitude and vast variety of sufferings which thy Saviour has endured for thee—from His entrance into the Garden of Gethsemane till His expiring on the Cross. View them one by one, and thou shalt see that not one part of His sacred body—which being the most perfect, was at the same time the most sensitive to pain of any that ever has been—was free from its peculiar torments. His head was crowned with thorns, His face defiled with spittle, all bruised and black with blows; His hair and beard plucked and torn; His mouth drenched with gall and vinegar; His shoulders oppressed with the weight of the Cross; His hands and feet pierced with nails; His whole body exhausted with a bloody sweat, mangled and laid open with whips and scourges; His limbs wearied out, and all disjointed upon the Cross. What He suffered in His soul was not one jot less, but rather infinitely more than what He suffered in His body. Witness that mortal anguish which cast Him into His Agony in the Garden; witness that grievous complaint on the Cross, *"My God, my God, why hast thou forsaken me?"* (*Matthew* 27:46). He suffered, moreover, in His reputation, which is often dearer to man than life, by false witnesses and outrageous calumnies and imputations; He suffered in His honor, by all kinds of reproaches and affronts; He suffered in His goods, being despoiled of His very clothes and hanging naked upon the Cross; He suffered in His friends, being forsaken by them all. This is not to speak of other sufferings, which are usually felt more by flesh and blood, viz., the ingratitude of those whom He had favored with His miracles, the triumphs of His enemies, their insults over His disciples, etc. And in all these sufferings, He denied Himself those comforts which He usually affords His servants under their crosses and which have made the greatest torments of the martyrs not only tolerable, but oftentimes sweet and comforting. But He would allow Himself no other comfort but that of doing the Will of His Father and purchasing our Redemption.

Consider fourthly who it is that suffers all this, and thou shalt find that He is the eternal Son of God, equal and consubstantial to His Father, the great Lord and Maker of Heaven and Earth, infinite in power, infinite in wisdom, infinite in all perfections. But for whom does He suffer all this? For poor man, a wretched worm of the earth; for ungrateful sinners, traitors to His Eternal Father and to Himself; for those very Jews who crucified Him; for us mortals who for the most part were never likely to thank Him or even so much as to think of His sufferings. Oh, how admirable art Thou, O Lord, in all Thy ways, but in none more than in the designs of Thy mercy! Oh, how does this Passion of our Redeemer set out and illustrate all the attributes of God! It is here that we discover His infinite goodness and charity, in thus wonderfully communicating Himself to us and laying down His own life for us. It is here that we discover His unparalleled mercy, in taking upon Himself our miseries and enduring the stripes due to our sins. Here we see the admirable wisdom of His Providence, in opening to us by His own death the fountain of life. Here we learn to fear His justice, which fell so heavily upon His own Son, who had but clothed Himself in the resemblance of a sinner in order to make atonement for our sins. Oh, what must the guilty themselves one day expect at His hands if they do not prevent the terrors of His justice by laying hold of His present mercy!

Consider fifthly, in the sufferings of thy Saviour, the infinite malice, the unparalleled heinousness of mortal sin, which was not to be cancelled except by the last drop of the blood of the Son of God. This is one of the chief lessons which thy Saviour desires to teach thee from the Cross. Thou canst not please Him better than by studying well this great lesson. Oh, never be so ungrateful as to crucify Him again by mortal sin! Oh, let not that monster live in thee, for the destroying of which, CHRIST Himself would die.

THE END

Rules of A Christian Life

To Be Observed By All That Desire to Secure to Themselves A Happy Eternity

1. Settle in your soul a firm resolution, on no account whatever to consent to mortal sin. This resolution is the very foundation of a virtuous life. Whosoever is not arrived thus far, has not yet begun to serve God. Without this resolution, it is in vain for anyone to flatter himself with the hopes of living holily or dying happily.

2. In order to enable yourself to keep this resolution, be diligent in fleeing from all dangerous occasions, such as bad company, lewd or profane books, immodest plays, etc. *"For he that loveth danger shall perish in it."* *(Ecclesiasticus 2:27).*

3. Watch all the motions of your heart, and resist the first impressions of evil; keep a guard upon your senses and your imagination, that the enemy may not surprise your soul by these avenues. Do not make light of small faults, lest by degrees you fall into greater ones.

4. Flee from an idle life as from the mother of all mischief, and take it for a certain truth that an idle life will never bring a Christian to Heaven.

5. Never omit, on any account, your morning and evening prayers. In the morning, remember always to present to God the first fruits of the day by giving Him

115

your first thoughts; make an offering to Him of all the actions of the day; and renew this oblation at the beginning of everything you do. *"Whether you eat or drink,"* says St. Paul, *"or whatsoever else you do, do all to the glory of God."* (*1 Corinthians* 10:31).

6. In your evening prayers, make a daily examination of your conscience, calling yourself to an account of how you have passed the day; and whatever sins you discover, labor to wash them away by penitential tears before you lay yourself down to sleep. Who knows but that this night may be your last. In going to bed, think of the grave; compose yourself to rest in the arms of your God; and if you awake in the night, raise your thoughts to Him who is always watching over you.

7. Besides your morning and evening devotions, set aside some time in the day for prayer, more particularly mental prayer, by an interior conversation of your soul with God, her only true and Sovereign Good. In the midst of all your employments, keep yourself as much as possible in the presence of God, and frequently raise your mind to Him by short aspirations. Frequently read spiritual books, as letters or messages sent to you from Heaven. And if your circumstances permit, assist daily at the Sacrifice of the Mass.

8. Frequent the Sacraments at least once a month,* and take special care to prepare yourself to receive them worthily.

---

*At the time Bishop Challoner wrote this piece of advice, the "Penal Laws" of England against the practice of Catholicism were still in effect and being enforced at least often enough to make life dangerous for Catholics. Therefore, Mass and the Sacraments were available then on a daily basis to relatively few. Also, by the mid-Eighteenth Century, there had developed in the Catholic Church a false sense of moderation about frequent reception of the Sacraments of Confession and Holy Communion, so that reception once a month was considered fairly "frequent." Under the influence of St. Alphonsus Liguori, a Doctor of the Church (1696-1787), "frequent"

9. Have a great devotion to the Passion of Christ, and often meditate upon His sufferings.

10. Be particularly devoted to His Blessed Mother; take her for your mother, and seek her protection and prayers on all occasions; but learn besides to imitate her virtues.

11. Study to find out your predominant passion, and labor with all your power to root it out.

12. Let not a day pass without offering to God some acts of contrition for past sins, and strive to maintain in your soul a penitential spirit.

13. Beware of self-love as your greatest enemy, and often use violence toward yourself by self-denial and mortification. Remember that the Kingdom of Heaven is not to be gained but by violence: *"The kingdom of Heaven suffereth violence, and the violent bear it away."* (*Matthew* 11:12).

14. Give alms according to your ability; *"For [there shall be] judgment without mercy to him that hath not done mercy."* (*James* 2:13). Set a great value upon spiri-

---

with regard to Confession and Holy Communion came to mean "at least weekly," a practice that was finally promoted worldwide by St. Pius X (1903-1914) and which obtained until just after Vatican Council II (1962-1965). At the time of this publication, once a month for Confession is generally considered "frequent," although this understanding of "frequent" does not seem to reflect the traditional, long-standing practice of the Church, for many Popes and great Saints went to Confession daily, such as St. Thomas Aquinas (1225-1274), a Doctor of the Church, and St. Vincent Ferrer (1350-1419), one of her greatest missionaries and miracle-workers, both of whom were considered never to have committed a mortal sin. People in high positions with great responsibility in the Church, the State, or even in the business world, are well advised to confess more frequently than once a week, as the great missionary bishop St. Anthony Mary Claret (1807-1870), who went to Confession several times a week. St. Francis Borgia (1510-1572), third general of the Jesuits, confessed twice a day! Daily Holy Communion is currently being urged and advised in the Church.

tual almsdeeds by striving all you can to reclaim un-happy sinners, and for that end daily bewail their misery in the sight of God.

15. Be exact in all the duties of your calling, as having to give an account one day to that great Master who has allotted to each one of us our respective station in His family.

16. *"In all thy works remember thy last end, and thou shalt never sin." (Ecclesiasticus 7:40).*

Appendix I

Prayers Proper To Be Recited By Those Who Desire To Amend Their Lives

Consider the danger to which you have been exposed— of losing your soul by your sins. Reflect upon the malice, the multitude and the ingratitude of your crimes, and upon the sufferings of your Saviour to expiate them. This done, consider in the next place the measures which you should henceforth adopt and pursue for the entire amendment of your life. Think seriously upon the occasions and dangers of sin to which you are exposed and upon the company which you should avoid. Endeavor to feel forcibly the necessity of forming strong and determined resolutions, for without these, no sorrow can be sincere and the hope of pardon, without them, is vain and illusive. Having therefore made these reflections, proceed and say the following prayers.

An Act of Contrition

ALMIGHTY and most merciful God, Thou hast long borne with me in my sins, and Thou hast long and often invited and pressed me to return to Thee once more. Behold, therefore, such is now my sincere desire. I now earnestly wish to quit the husks of swine and to return home to the house of my Father, in the full hope of obtaining pardon from Thy mercy. I desire to come now before Thee, my God, with a contrite heart and to make at Thy feet a sincere acknowledgment of all my sins and offenses.

Wherefore, prostrating myself humbly before Thee, I here confess the greatness of my ingratitude to Thee and the multitude of my crimes, and I earnestly implore Thy pardon. I am indeed the prodigal child who has long gone astray from Thee, squandering away my substance and seeking, but seeking in vain, to satisfy my appetite with empty satisfactions. Being now, however, made aware of my own misery and weary of my evil ways, I anxiously wish to return again to Thee. I confess myself unworthy to be called Thy child, and what I now crave of Thy mercy is Thy forgiveness. I am afraid even to lift up my eyes toward Thee, and much less to ask a place, although it were the lowest in Thy family. I feel myself loaded and oppressed with the weight of my disorders, which I now detest from the bottom of my heart.

Do Thou then, O Father of Mercies, have pity and compassion on me. Look not upon my sins, but upon the sufferings and the merits of my Redeemer. Look upon Him and upon all that He has done and endured for my salvation. Oh mercy, mercy, by those tears which He shed for me in Gethsemane and by that blood which He spilled for me upon the Cross, I here lay down all my sins to be washed away by this sacred stream!

Yes, my God, I am sincerely sorry for all my past negligences and offenses. I wish that, like the Magdalen, I could wash the feet of my Saviour with penitential tears. I wish I could wash away my sins, although it were even with the tears of blood. In Thy mercy, however, forgive me. Cleanse my soul from all its stains, and let nothing henceforth—no temptation nor fraud of the enemy—so far prevail over me as to be able ever to separate me from Thy love, through Jesus Christ, our Lord. *Amen.*

Another Act of Contrition

I AM confounded, O my God, at the sight of my sins and at the ingratitude with which I have treated Thy goodness toward me. I am confounded to think that I have fallen so often and so easily into the same offenses, after having so often and so solemnly promised that I would not commit them anymore. How, indeed, could I ever have brought myself, for the sake of such empty and trifling satisfactions, to rebel against Thee, my God—above all, knowing as well as I do how hateful all sin is in Thy sight and abusing Thy blessings in order to insult Thee? O Father of Mercies, Thou tenderest and best of parents, allow Thy just displeasure against me to be appeased. Punish me not according to the rigor of Thy justice, but in the kindness of Thy compassion, forgive me. *Amen.*

An Act of Resolution

I T was my duty to have sacrificed everything, even life itself, rather than to have sinned against Thee, my God. But since such, alas, has been my misfortune, and since the past is no longer mine, I am at least now firmly resolved, by the help of Thy grace, to be henceforth so watchful over myself as to do nothing that may lead me back into my former sins. For this end, I will carefully shun all those dangers and occasions, all those places and persons, which have been the cause of my relapses. Above all, I will be particularly watchful over my predominant passion, and I will manfully resist all those temptations and avoid all those offenses into which, through habit, weakness or inclination, I have been betrayed and seduced into sin most easily. For this purpose, moreover, I will assiduously make use of those measures of security which shall be suggested to me by Thy minister in the tribunal of Confession. I will attend to his counsels and directions as coming from Thee, because it is in reality to Thee that I answer and to Thee that I promise, in the answers and the promises which I make to him. In short, I now firmly propose for the time to come, no more to offend Thee, renouncing from this day every sinful pleasure and every criminal desire. I will, moreover, make what satisfaction I am able to Thy justice—if not by a life of painful mortification, at least by a life of piety and love, through Jesus Christ Our Lord. *Amen.*

A Prayer to Beg the Intercession of Our Lady and the Saints before Confession

MAY the blessed Angels and Saints of God, who rejoice in the conversion of a sinner; and above all, may thou, O Blessed Virgin, the refuge of the penitent and the Mother of Mercies, intercede for me, that the Confession which I am now going to make may not have the effect of rendering me more criminal than I am, but may procure for me the happiness of a reconciliation with my long-offended God and the grace never more to offend Him mortally.

And do thou, likewise, my good Angel, the faithful guardian of my soul and the witness of my past sins and infidelities—do thou, by thy prayers, assist me to rise again and beg that, in this holy Sacrament, I may obtain those helps which may enable me to lead a new life for the time to come. *Amen.*

The Penitent's Litany

Have mercy on me, O God, according to Thy great mercy.
And according to the multitude of Thy tender mercies, blot out my iniquity. (Psalm 50:3).
Lord, have mercy on me.
　　Christ, have mercy on me.
God the Father of Heaven, *Have mercy on me.*
God the Son, Redeemer of the world, *Have mercy on me.*
God the Holy Ghost, Perfecter of the elect, *etc.*

Holy Trinity, one God, *etc.*

O God, Who by the voice of Thy prophets and Apostles dost call upon us incessantly to be converted and to abandon our evil ways,

O Divine Saviour, Jesus Christ, Who didst Thyself come on earth to call sinners to repentance,

O Jesus, the Good Shepherd, Who didst come among us to seek and to save the lost sheep,

O Jesus, Who hast declared that unless we do penance, we shall perish everlastingly,

O Jesus, Who desirest not the death of the sinner, but that he be converted and live,

O Jesus, Who hast assured us that there shall be joy in Heaven over one sinner that is converted and does penance,

O Jesus, Who, in the example of the prodigal son returning home to the bosom of his father, hast inspired us with confidence in Thy tenderness,

O Jesus, Who for the sake and salvation of sinners wast pleased to undergo so many hardships, labors and fatigues,

O Jesus, Who didst not refuse to receive publicans and public sinners, in order to draw them to repentance,

O Jesus, Who callest upon us to be converted to Thee with all our hearts,

Have mercy upon me, O Lord, and hear my prayer.
Have mercy upon me, O Lord, and hear my petition.

From all evil, *Deliver me, O Lord.*

From all sin, *Deliver me, O Lord.*

From the spirit of impenitence and from all hardness of heart, *etc.*

From final impenitence, *etc.*

By Thy baptism and holy fasting,

By Thy labors and sorrows,

By the merits of Thy Precious Blood, which Thou hast shed for my sins,

On the Day of Judgment,

That Thou would vouchsafe in Thy mercy to create in me
a new heart and a new mind, *I beseech Thee to hear me,
O Lord.*

That Thou would vouchsafe to conduct me to true repentance, *I beseech Thee to hear me, O Lord.*

That as I have imitated the Prodigal in his sins, so may I
also imitate him in his sorrow, *etc.*

That as I am the lost sheep, so Thou, as the Good Shepherd, deign kindly to carry me back to the fold upon
Thy shoulders,

That as hitherto I have served iniquity unto iniquity, so
henceforth I may serve justice unto sanctification,

That I may cultivate all the virtues of the truly penitent
and bring forth fruits worthy of piety,

That for the time to come, renouncing all impiety and
worldly desires, I may live chastely, soberly and inno-
cently,

That Thou wilt give me the grace and courage to resist
my passions, to bend my will to obedience to Thy laws,
and to crucify my flesh with its vices and concupis-
cences,

That, like the prudent virgins in the Gospel, I may be
always watchful, that I may cherish prayer and that I
may cultivate industry,

That I may with confidence have recourse to the throne
of grace, that thus I may obtain grace in seasonable
aid,

That Thou wouldst not deal with me according to my
sins, but in Thine infinite tenderness, have pity upon
me,

That I may so purify myself by penance and by the sufferings of this life as to avoid those torments which
are reserved for the impenitent hereafter,

O Lamb of God, Who takest away the sins of the world,
Spare me, O Lord.

O Lamb of God, Who takest away the sins of the world,

Graciously hear me, O Lord.
O Lamb of God, Who takest away the sins of the world,
Have mercy upon me, O Lord.

Let Us Pray

O God, Who willest not the death of the sinner, but that he be converted and live, vouchsafe in Thy mercy to look down in compassion upon my misery and my weakness, in order that, remembering that I am only dust and ashes and that soon, in punishment for my sins, I must return to dust and ashes again, I may thus be prepared to receive the pardon of my manifold offenses and receive that recompense which Thou hast promised to the penitent, through Jesus Christ Our Lord. *Amen.*

O Father of Mercies and Tender Physician of our Souls, I have grievously sinned against Thee, and I am no longer worthy to be called Thy child. I have repaid Thy benefits with ingratitude and Thy graces with neglect. I have merited Thy displeasure and have deserved the heavy weight of Thy punishments. Deeply aware of this, my unhappy state, behold, I now present myself before Thee to implore Thy pardon. Pardon me then, O God of Love, and remember not the sins of my past life. Remember only that Thou art my Father and that I am still Thy child. Thy mercy still exceeds the greatness of my misery. Wherefore, O God, unworthy sinner that I am, I will not cease to confide in Thee. In Thee, O Lord, I have trusted; let me not be confounded forever. I propose from henceforth daily to bewail my past ingratitude, and I now make at Thy feet the firm resolution never more to offend Thee mortally, and to fly with the most prudent care from all those occasions which I know by experience are dangerous to my weakness. By the help of Thy grace, I will adopt the securest means of overcoming my passions and of subduing my evil habits, through Jesus Christ Our Lord. *Amen.*

Appendix II

Instructions and Devotions For the Sick

Q. *When a person is seized with sickness, what ought to be his chief concern?*

A. To consider the state of his soul and resolve upon using all the means proper for making his peace with God and putting himself in such a condition that, if Almighty God shall please to call him out of this world, he may not be found unprepared. No delays ought to be admitted in this regard, because to prepare for *dying well* is a great work; they who have lived well have made the surest preparation for it; and yet, even these too will find enough to do in the time of their sickness to prepare their souls for this last passage. How much more, then, will those have upon their hands who in their lives have foresaken God and been neglectful of many Christian duties? As for such who have thus lived in sin and on their deathbed seem to return to God and ask for mercy, I must say, with many Fathers, their case is very dangerous, if not desperate; I can promise nothing in return for such late endeavors, which are very seldom sincere. However, since none ought to despair, I wish all sorts would make the best use of their sickness, which is a call from Heaven to prepare themselves for eternity. Those who have lived best will certainly go on with the greater confidence in God; and as for the others, who knows but that God may also show mercy to them?

First, then, let the sick person, while he sends for the physician, or such as may take care of his health, remember also to call for his spiritual physician, the priest, who can help to put his soul in a good state.

Secondly, let him induce his best friends to reveal to him the danger of his illness as soon as they become aware of it and ask them not to flatter him with the hopes of recovery when in reality there appears none, that thus he may dispose his soul for what God has appointed for him and not be surprised by a sudden and unexpected death. For it is most certainly a very unfriendly act to delude a sick person with false hopes, and on the pretext of not disturbing him, to take out of his hands the opportunity—never more to be recovered—of preparing his soul to appear before his Lord. This is a sort of friendship that is very barbarous and cruel, that for preserving of a short peace is ventured the loss of that which is eternal.

Thirdly, if he has not his will already made (as in prudence he ought), let him be careful in the beginning of his sickness to call for such experienced persons as may help him to make it, that thus having settled all temporal affairs, he may wholly apply his thoughts afterwards, without any disturbance, to the care of his soul. Thus it is that many otherwise good people are very much preoccupied, neglecting to make their wills in time of health, as if they were afraid to think of dying, and then still putting it off in time of sickness, so that as too often happens, they either die without a will, or else make it in such disorder that they entail on their friends and relations lasting contentions and endless expenses, which might have been prevented by their timely care, and it will most certainly be severely laid to their charge, since by their willful neglect, they have given the occasion of these disorders and scandals.

Fourthly, if he be in debt or has any restitution to make, let him take care to satisfy these obligations to the best of his power.

Fifthly, let him be mindful to forgive all those who have in any way injured him and to beg pardon of as many as he has wronged, either in word or deed.

Sixthly, if the illness be dangerous, let him admit but few visits, since the conversation of most people is only so much distraction and helps to bring the world into one who is going out of it.

The reason why these things ought to be done in the beginning of sickness is that many illnesses unexpectedly affect the mind and deprive a man of all reason and judgment; and where the disease spares the brain, the physician very often does not, prescribing remedies which put him under such a dozing sleepiness that it may be he never again truly comes to himself, but goes out of this world sleeping and senseless. Thus, whether from the disease or from the remedy, an opportunity of settling these affairs, which was lost in the beginning, too often proves past all recovery and therefore in prudence ought not to be neglected.

Q. *After the sick man has reason to hope that he has effectually made his peace with God, what method do you propose to be used as most proper to prepare him for his last hour and to fit him to appear before his Judge?*

A. There can be no one method fit for all, but a great deal must be left to discretion, in compliance with particular cases and circumstances. But though it is most certain, however, that a soul without true faith in God, without hope and confidence in His goodness, without charity, without a sincere repentance, without resignation, patience, etc., is very unfit to be presented before the Judgment Seat; therefore, it is absolutely necessary in time of sickness that care should be taken to establish a soul in these virtues, that thus being purified from all sin, it may be found clothed in its wedding garments, and thus enter into eternity. A good director and pious books will be helpful to achieve this end, but for those souls such as are not better provided, I will here set down a short collection of devotions by which it may be in the power of any charitable friend to assist his neighbor in doing this great work—which being once well done, will be an everlasting blessing.

A Prayer in the Beginning of any Illness

LORD Jesus Christ, behold I receive this illness which Thou art pleased to give me from Thy fatherly hand. It is Thy Will for me, and therefore I accept it. Thy Will be done on earth, as it is in Heaven. May it be to the honor of Thy holy Name and the good of my soul. For this purpose I here offer myself with an entire submission to all Thy designs, to suffer whatever Thou dost please, as long as Thou dost please, and in what manner Thou dost please. For I am Thy creature, O Lord, who have most ungratefully offended Thee. And since my sins have for a long time called aloud to Heaven for justice, why shall I now complain if I feel Thy hand upon me? No, my God, Thou art just in all Thy ways; I have truly deserved Thy punishments, and therefore I have no reason to complain of Thee, but only of my own wickedness.

But correct me not, O Lord, I beseech Thee, in Thine anger, but have regard for my weakness. Thou knowest how frail I am, that I am nothing but dust and ashes. Deal not with me, therefore, according to my sins, nor punish me according to my iniquities, but according to the multitude of Thy most tender mercies, have compassion on me. Let Thy mercy come mixed with Thy justice, and let Thy grace be my support in my illness. Confirm my soul with strength from above, that I may bear with patience all the uneasiness, pain, disquietude and difficulties of my illness, and that I may cheerfully accept them as the just punishment of my offenses. Preserve me from all temptations, and be Thou my defense against all assaults of the enemy, that in this illness I may in no way offend Thee. And if this is to be my last illness, I beg of Thee so to direct me by Thy grace that I may in no way neglect or be deprived of those means which Thou hast in Thy mercy ordained for the good of my soul, to prepare it for its passage into eternity; that being perfectly cleansed from all my iniquities, I may believe in Thee, love Thee, put my whole trust in Thee, and through the merits of Thy Passion and Death, be admitted into the company of the Blessed, where I may praise Thee forever. *Amen.*

This, or similar prayers, ought to be said, at least in heart, not only in the beginning, but every day throughout the whole time of illness.

SPIRITUAL EXERCISES

Spiritual Exercises proper in any long illness, to be read periodically, leisurely and distinctly, by any friend, whom the sick person may accompany, not in words, but in heart.

An Act of Faith

I BELIEVE in God, the Father Almighty, Who has made me to His own image and likeness; and in Jesus Christ, my Saviour, Who has redeemed me by His Precious Blood; and in the Holy Ghost, Who has sanctified me in my Baptism.

I believe the Holy Catholic Church and whatever she teaches, as received from Christ and His Apostles. Of this Church I profess myself at present to be a member, and thus I desire to die.

In profession of this Faith, I here recite the Apostles' Creed:

The Apostles' Creed

I believe in God, the Father Almighty, Creator of Heaven and earth; and in Jesus Christ, His only Son, Our Lord, Who was conceived by the Holy Ghost, born of the Virgin Mary, suffered under Pontius Pilate, was crucified, died and was buried. He descended into Hell; the third day He arose again from the dead; He ascended into Heaven, sitteth at the right hand of God, the Father Almighty; from thence He shall come to judge the living and the dead. I believe in the Holy Ghost, the Holy Catholic Church, the Communion of Saints, the forgiveness of sins, the Resurrection of the Body, and life everlasting. *Amen.*

All of these truths I understand in the sense our Holy Mother the Church has always understood them. Thus, O God, I believe; increase, I beseech Thee, and confirm my faith. With this profession of faith in my heart, I desire to appear before Thy tribunal, where I firmly hope I shall see the good things which Thou hast prepared in the land of the living.

An Act of Hope

THOU hast prepared, O Lord, everlasting happiness for those who love Thee. But how can I expect a part in this reward—I, who am a most grievous sinner and who from my childhood have ever done evil in Thy sight? Ah, my God, while I look on myself, I am terrified by my sins and see there nothing but reasons for despair. And from this sense of my own unworthiness, I here declare I have nothing of my own to trust in: no, my God, nothing of my own to trust in, but all my hope is in Thee!

I confess, therefore, that my sins are many and grievous; but still, I trust in Thy mercy, that through the Passion and merits of my Redeemer, Jesus Christ, I shall obtain pardon of my offenses and partake of the glory of the Blessed. Thou hast said it, O Lord, that Thou wilt cast off none that place their hope in Thee: Behold I hope in Thee; let me not be confounded forever. Though I were guilty of many more sins, yet still would I trust in Thee, for Thy mercy is infinitely above all my iniquity.

Look on me therefore with the eyes of compassion, and reject not the petition of one prostrate at Thy feet. I am dust and ashes, but behold I offer to Thee the Passion and Blood of Thy only Son; in these I have an infinite treasure of mercy stored up for me. He laid down His life for sinners and became a propitiation for my offenses. It is this which I now present to Thee; it is on this and Thy promises that I ground all my hope; and since I have this to depend on, I will never despair, but ever preserve a firm and lively trust in Thee.

Our Lord is my light and my salvation; whom shall I fear? Our Lord is my protector, and nothing shall hurt me. Our Lord is merciful and full of compassion; as a tender father has compassion on his children, so will Our Lord show mercy to all who fear Him, for He knows what we are and of what we are made. He is sweet and tender to all, and His mercies are above all His works. He gives strength to the weak, raises up those that fall, comforts the afflicted and pardons sinners. O God, all these good effects I hope Thou wilt at present work in my soul, and so watch over me that nothing necessary for my salvation shall be wanting to me. *Amen.*

An Act of Charity

I LOVE Thee, my Lord God, and it is my hearty desire to increase still more and more in Thy love, that I may love Thee as Thou hast commanded, with all my heart, with all my soul, and with all my strength. Thou art to me all in all, and outside of Thee there is nothing able to help me or that is worthy of my love. O Infinite Goodness, when shall I perfectly love Thee? When wilt Thou wholly possess my heart? When shall I be entirely Thine? Oh, let that happy hour come when Thou wilt take full possession of my heart, that I may give myself wholly to Thee. Lord Jesus Christ, Thou hast bestowed infinite blessings upon me throughout the whole course of my life; add this one blessing more, I beseech Thee, to all the former—that I may here perfectly renounce all the unlawful, vain and unprofitable affections of this world and begin now to fix my heart on Thee with a pure and perfect love which may abide for all eternity. *Amen.*

An Act of Patience

I WILL speak to Our Lord, I who am but dust and ashes and as the shadow that passes away. Remember, O Lord, what I am, and what my being is. Remember that Thou hast made me out of clay, and unto earth I shall return again. Show not therefore Thy power against me, for what strength have I to bear it? And how shall I, being so weak as I am, hold out with patience? Why then has my Lord stretched forth His hand against me and let this disorder seize on my spirits and cast me on the bed of sickness? But rather, why do I now lift up my head against Heaven and appear uneasy under the decrees of the Almighty? No, I will rather choose to say that it is Our Lord Who has given health and strength; it is Our Lord Who has taken it away; as it has seemed good to Our Lord, so be it done. Blessed be the name of Our Lord. Thus I say, my God; thus I think. Thou art just, O Lord; Thy judgment is right; I have deserved far greater punishment than this. Were I to be my own judge and the punisher of my own wickedness, I could take nothing off of the evil which I now suffer. In what I feel, I acknowledge the hand of a tender Father, chastising a rebellious child; it is not the arm of a severe judge, punishing me in the justice of his wrath. But this one thing, O merciful Father, I ask of Thee however: that Thou wouldst remember what I am: that I am frail and weak, that of myself I can do nothing and how much I stand in need of Thy grace to support and comfort me. Grant me, therefore, I beseech Thee, strength to suffer; give me patience, for this is necessary for me. Grant this my request, and then behold my heart is ready, O Lord; my heart is ready to accept whatever Thou art pleased to lay upon me—and even to be comforted under Thy scourge. Let it be the effect of Thy mercy, that in patience I may possess my soul. For this end I will often look on the face of Thy Christ, that by considering Him Who suffered so much for me, I may be encouraged to suffer. He became obedient unto death, even to the death of the Cross. But as for me, I have not yet resisted unto blood; I have yet suffered but little. Yet how much shall I then suffer when the time shall come when the pangs of death shall seize upon me!

An Act of Resignation

O LORD Jesus Christ, Thou art my refuge; in Thee I believe and put my trust. Thou hast been my protector from my youth, and now I have none to trust in, none to depend upon, but only Thee, my God. Behold then, the straits I am now in: I have life and death before me, but what to fear or what to hope I know not. I know not what is expedient or best for me; Thou knowest, O Jesus. Do Thou with me, therefore, what Thou dost please; dispose of me as Thou knowest best, for I am Thine with all my heart, and into Thy hands I surrender all that I have or am. *Amen.*

About the Author

(Adapted from "Richard Challoner" by Edwin Burton, *The Catholic Encyclopedia*, Vol. 3, pages 564-566. Robert Appleton Co., New York, N.Y.,1908.)

The Most Reverend Doctor Richard Challoner was born September 29, 1691 of Presbyterian parents in Sussex, England. Upon his father's death, his mother became the housekeeper of a Catholic family named Gage at Firle in Sussex. It is unknown if she became a Catholic prior to this or during her service with them. In any event, Richard was received into the Church at age 13, in Warkworth, Northamptonshire, where Fr. John Gother, chaplain to George Holman, Esq. and Lady Holman, Catholics, instructed him in the Catholic Faith and procured a nomination for him at Douay College in France, which he entered at age 14 in 1705, spending the next 25 years there in various capacities, until age 39. He completed the usual 12 years' course in only 8 years. At 21, he was chosen to teach rhetoric and poetry, and a year later he was appointed professor of philosophy, a post he held for eight years.

Ordained a priest on March 28, 1716, he graduated as a Bachelor of Divinity in 1719 and in 1720 was chosen by Dr. Witham, president of the University of Douay to be his vice-president, and he also became professor of theology and prefect of studies. In 1727 he received the degree of Doctor of Divinity and in 1728, he published his first book, *Think Well On't*. In 1730 he returned to London to

135

embrace the pastoral ministry. Due to the Penal Laws against Catholics being still in effect in England and sporadically enforced (there was a £100 reward for the conviction of a priest), priests had to wear secular garb and say Mass and administer the Sacraments in private. In 1738 he published *The Catholic Christian Instructed in the Sacraments, Sacrifice and Ceremonies of the Church*, the preface of which answered an Anglican theologian who had attacked the Church. This writer resented Dr. Challoner's reply and set the law in motion against him, such that he was forced to leave England and return to Douay that year. Dr. Witham, president of Douay, having died about that time, efforts were made to appoint Dr. Challoner president of the University there. But the Bishop of London, Dr. Petre, desired him to be his Coadjutor Bishop. Though opposing his own elevation to the episcopacy, Dr. Challoner was nonetheless appointed and was consecrated bishop on January 29, 1741. During three years, he made a methodical visit to his entire ten-county English diocese, plus the Channel Islands, the first complete visitation since 1688. The district also included all the English-held colonies in America and some of the West Indian islands, none of which he was ever able to visit. In 1758, Dr. Petre died and Bishop Challoner succeeded him as Bishop of the London district. By then, however, he was 67 and very ill, so that a new Coadjutor Bishop, James Talbot, had to be appointed to this office.

Despite his heavy pastoral duties, Bishop Challoner also continued to write books: In 1740, he issued *The Garden of the Soul*, a prayerbook and his most famous book. Next was *Memoirs of Missionary Priests*, an account of the English martyrs from 1577-1681, and in 1745 *Britannia Sancta*, the lives of the English, Irish and Scottish Saints. In 1749 he issued the first edition of his updated Douay-Rheims New Testament, in 1750 the second edition of the New Testament plus the first edition of the Old Testament, then in 1752 a thoroughly re-edited version of the whole Bible. "Dr. Challoner's Bible has been the groundwork of nearly all subsequent English versions," (Edwin Burton), and of his literary works the one that has had by far the greatest impact on the English-speaking world. In 1753 he issued the popular *Meditations for Every Day of the Year*, and *British Martyrology* in 1761. He has also made probably the best English translation of *The Imitation of Christ*, plus he wrote a *Catechism of Christian Doctrine*, and some 25 other books. Bishop Richard Challoner died on January 12, 1781 at age almost 90, after a life of prodigious activity on behalf of the Catholic Church and of souls—both through his pastoral ministry and his writing, all the while dodging the law and the 18th-Century English equivalent of priest "bounty-hunters."

Considering Bishop Challoner's life and work, and those of so many great missionaries and Saints, one can see that our Faith was planted, nurtured and fostered by giants among men, whose work—throughout most of the Church and the world—remains largely unknown and unappreciated.

If you have enjoyed this book, consider making your next selection from among the following . . .

Prices subject to change.

Prices subject to change.

At your Bookdealer or direct from the Publisher.

Toll-Free 1-800-437-5876   ***Fax 815-226-7770***
Tel. 815-226-7777   ***www.tanbooks.com***

Prices subject to change.

GIVE

THINK WELL ON IT

To those you know who would benefit from this dynamite little book. There is probably no other book in English that better summarizes the message of Our Lord's Gospel than **Think Well On It**—or better admonishes the reader to rectify his life and save his soul while there is still time. For our great and merciful God has allotted to each person a certain segment of time during which he can easily obtain forgiveness for his sins, expiate them with relative ease, and begin to lead the joy-filled life of a true Christian, whose conscience is clear and who is living in the certitude that he is on the right path to Heaven.

As Our Lord's Gospel is for everyone, everyone—man, woman and child, Catholic and non-Catholic alike—stands to benefit from this compelling book. Search Christian literature over, and you will undoubtedly never find so persuasive a book as **Think Well On It** to bring a person to the realization of just what it is that Our Lord is teaching us in the Gospel that we must do to save our souls from Hell and an eternal now of suffering, yet at so small a price, purchase an eternity of unending joy in the presence of God, Our Lord Jesus Christ, His Blessed Mother, St. Joseph and all the Saints and Angels—where *"Eye hath not seen, nor ear heard, neither hath it entered into the heart of man what things God has prepared for them that love Him."* (*1 Corinthians 2:9*).

Now is the time to act; *now* is the time unabashedly to present those you know and love with this incomparable but relatively brief book, with its message of repentance and reform, stated as no one else has so contrived to state the message of the Gospel. *"And we, helping, do exhort you, that you receive not the grace of God in vain. For he saith: 'In an accepted* time have I heard thee, and in the day of salvation have I helped thee.' Behold, now is the acceptable time; behold now is the day of salvation." (2 Corinthians 6:2).

No one knows how much time God has granted him to live and to work out his salvation. When the Spirit speaks to us, therefore, *that* is the time to act, *that* is the time to effect our own cure, *that* is the time to help others. Yes, *that* is the time to give this book to others! The soul you save may very well be your own. *"My brethren, if any of you err from the truth, and one convert him, he must know that he who causeth a sinner to be converted from the error of his way, shall save his soul from death, and shall cover a multitude of sins." (James 5:19-20).*

Act now, while the spirit moves you. Do not be ashamed to give this book to others. You will be glad you did. And remember Our Lord's stirring words, *"Everyone therefore that shall confess me before men, I will also confess him before my Father who is in heaven." (Matthew 10:32).*

God will bless you for whatever you do!

Quantity Discounts

Copies	Each	Sh/Hdlg	Total
1 copy	$12.00	+5.00	17.00
2 copies	9.00 ea.	+5.00	23.00
5 copies	7.00 ea.	+5.00	41.00
10 copies	6.00 ea.	+6.00	66.00
25 copies	5.00 ea.	+8.00	133.00

Illinois residents add 7% sales tax.

TAN BOOKS AND PUBLISHERS, INC.

P.O. Box 424, Rockford, Illinois 61105

1-800-437-5876 • FAX 815-226-7770

WWW.TANBOOKS.COM